To Terryl, Marilyn, Greg, Rob and Duncan who teach and share life's joy with me.

About The Author

Gary L. McDonald was an ordinary kid playing baseball and hockey after he learned to knit five finger gloves in his little fort at five years of age. He could add columns of numbers faster than the wind could blow at eight; he couldn't sing a note and wasn't very good with a violin at fifteen, so he quit all of that and began learning to print at sixteen. For his next 41 years he learned to: stay the course, focus on the work, seek proven human resources, cultivate business associates, and finally learn that quality books are printed for a purpose: to be read. He loved sports, eventually he grew to love his work, and after 57 years he attended a school of higher learning. He enjoyed York University for six years and then it was time to write and travel. He is not about to quit again.

Table of Contents

Gary McDonald, a former printer, sales person, sales manager, co-owner, president and general manager of Arthurs Jones Lithographing Ltd. (Pictured retiring on June 12, 1998) can be reached at garymcdonald12@rogers.com

Chapter One

I'm reaching back to a time in our lives that is vitally important to all of us. My memory is quite good. Perhaps you and I have been more fortunate than many in our lives who have lost a little or all of the ability to recall. Memory loss is a tragic condition that affects about 40% of us who will have some form of memory loss after turning 65. In the last eight years of my life, my physical abilities spiralled right down the rabbit hole, requiring hospital care with a few unrelated surgeries and more importantly, E.C.T. treatments with follow-up medication creating the stability I enjoy today. It's amazing. My memory loss involves pockets of my time while in the hospital and for example, vacations to places that I cannot remember. And by the way, there is a fellow named *Alexander McPope* whose name will creep into this book. He will sound like me because he IS me. He has been helping me with Refinement and Inspiration for 25 years.

How I Started to Print

I WAS BORN on September 1, 1941, under the horoscope sign quite applicable to me: Virgo. So too were Edgar Rice Burroughs (born in 1875) who wrote: "I write to escape...to escape poverty." and Rocky Marciano (1923) who said: "What would be better than walking down any street in any city and knowing you're a champion?" and Lily Tomlin (1939) who made us all laugh with lines like: "The trouble with the rat race is that even if you win, you're still a rat." Perhaps the only entity Burroughs, Marciano, Tomlin and I have in common is our birth date. We all have, or once had a vocation, a pursuit, a calling or line of work, but few write about it. This is my story—warts and all.

Mother (Emma J. [Arsenault] McDonald) and I went to St. Michael's Hospital in Toronto, where I first appeared. Dad rode in the taxi with us. Dad (James A. McDonald) revelled in the sentence: "He was born of poor but proud parents who were married on his fourteenth birthday." For that matter, he liked to say that about many people, in jest mind you; I've been heard to repeat that line as well. My birth date was Labour Day, September 1, 1941: the first Monday in September, three months and six days before the name Pearl Harbor spewed from radio and print. On December 7, 1941, the world's governments were at war against someone, anyone and almost everyone. This story is more about me, a very small speck in the grand scheme of things. When Dad told the boys at work of my arrival, one of them, clearly a friend, promised to work an entire shift for him if he would agree to name me Garfield. That generous offer came from a certain lathe operator whose name was Garfield. When Dad presented his selection of one name to Mom, he probably didn't include any agreement he made with any benevolent character at the factory. Mom's side of this tale is that her understanding of the name Gary was an abbreviation of Garfield. That makes sense. So it was written that I would be Garfield on paper and Gary in person. And Dad accepted an extra night's sleep on the job as his bonus.

This story and others that include me or anyone other than me before I reached the age of four are provided indirectly and come from others, who, in truth or lie, passed it on to me. Everything I recall on and after September 1, 1945, is gospel; and so my story begins with my earliest recollection and a chocolate birthday cake with lemon-flavoured filling between the layers, a party of kids and a guy named Wayne; Fink was his last name. Honest.

My mother made and served this masterpiece to my honoured four-year-old guests in my backyard, which was directly in front of a big empty lot overgrown with grass and very large Maple trees; we called it 'The Big Yard.' Sammy Long's Dad owned the big house we lived in, and I'll bet he owned the big yard as well. That house—our house, across the street from the Catholic school, twenty yards north of the Catholic Church and directly adjacent to the big yard—housed two large families: mine on the first floor with Mom and Dad and five kids, and Dad's younger brother Fred who was married to Mom's older sister Anna and their four kids on the second floor. The one washroom on the second floor was a busy room. In 1945 the oldest kid (Archie) was six, and the youngest (Danny) was just born. We climbed the huge trees in the big yard, we swung from tires strung from trees in the big yard, and some of us fell from those trees in the big yard, but no one died in the big yard that I know of; and come to think of it, no one I knew had died in the war either. Wayne and Sammy and Brackett and Willie and Knobby and Cully and Spike and HeyYou and Putt and Weed and Jack, Dan and Jeanette and dozens more were growing up all around the big yard, and so was I with no idea of what was happening around the world. We were happy and fed; what else was there? Wayne has long since disappeared (the Finks moved to California right after my birthday). The only thing I remember about Wayne Fink is his name.

All this, to add focus.

So, my story took place in the changing seasons of the east end of Toronto, where my dad (older people called him Arch) had toiled as a lathe operator during the war. (We fantasized about the bullets and tanks he made for the war effort.) At the beginning of the war, he enlisted in the armed forces but was denied due to a bronchial chest he had his entire life. Incredibly so, Dad, living with poor health and bad habits for almost as long as I've known him, celebrated his 92nd birthday in good spirits on December 9, 2002. My mother, a rock of Gibraltar with very soft shoulders for everyone she has ever known, blessed with good health and agreeable habits, celebrated her 87th birthday with a smile for all of us on August 12, 2002.

In the latter years of the 1940's swimming in Lake Ontario was a healthy pursuit. Unfortunately, that can't be said of the warmish polluted water of our lake today. We had bicycles that took us there in twenty minutes. On frozen days in winter, ice and road hockey were

3

our sports. On wet fall and spring days, our favourite pastimes were just a few days away. Our days were full with school, church, sewer tag, burby, hardball, road hockey, forts built close to the big yard, and Sammy blowing up live frogs with a straw. If it is true that we are what we eat, we never ate frogs, especially after Sammy was through with them.

We can be the games we play, the comics we read, the movies we see, the books that we read and the children of collected influence guiding or misguiding various epiphanies throughout our youth. In my case, I am one of your standard-bred, part Irish, part French, Catholic, average-sized people who did reasonably well in grade and high school without working at it. With 'little real effort' was the part that always annoyed my older brother (Richard) who worked hard and excelled at school. When he graduated from university, he was the first and only one of a long line of McDonalds and our buddies to accomplish this distinction prior to the 1970's. So at the age of 15 years and 11 months (1957) I blurted that I was through with Latin and Greek and Algebra and English in the middle of my public high school education. Rich was furious and said something like: "You're nuts—school could be so easy and rewarding for you if you worked at it and developed a passion for learning. You should read more, and I don't mean the sports pages either." But who listens to older brothers? That moment in my youth was strange, so strange that I've never totally understood it even to this day and neither did the coach at the playground or a couple of my high school teachers. My epiphany hit home in 1957 when I quit organized hockey, organized sandlot hardball and organized schoolwork to do something else. I had no idea what that 'something' was going to be three days short of my sixteenth birthday, but I was moving on. It has been said that waiting for a teenage boy to have some common sense is like holding a broomstick and waiting for flowers to sprout. Since that day, I have, on suitable occasion, characterized my intentions as one whereby money, a car and a babe were my priorities. I was very young when I was young.

4

Looking backward is the occupation of this narrative. I currently see my first sixteen years as comfortable; I enjoyed friendships and a questionable confidence that grew out of better-than-average accomplishments in sports but not much in anything else. Perhaps you remember your days of growing—heady days between the ages of eight to sixteen years of age—only eight years from a mathematical viewpoint, but so vital in many ways.

I was 105 pounds and around five feet plus four inches tall at fourteen years old and remained that size until I left the school system at sixteen. Why did that size and shape matter? It didn't affect my participation on the basketball team or the hockey team or the baseball team—I was good at these sports during grade school at St. Joseph's. It did however present a major challenge when I felt the urge to dance with one of the girls in my grade nine class at Riverdale Collegiate. She was blonde, cute and played the base violin—that's the big one that you stand to play—while I played the small one tucked under your chin. How did my fellow students get so tall and well-developed? I was only a year or so younger than the rest of the class, due in some manner to Miss Wallace, an extraordinary white-haired teacher who taught me to add columns of four-digit figures faster than I could speak the individual numbers. This took place in grade three, and this accomplishment, certainly one of significance, gave Miss Wallace an opportunity to elevate me to grade four in her combined classroom and complete the two years in one. Perhaps this was a way of moving students through the system faster, and therefore, a credit to the teacher as well as the system. Oh yeah, I could add like the wind could blow, but I didn't grow in size like the others. It wasn't a problem until I met the female base violinists in high school who were a head taller than me; you can imagine where that put my nose when they played Begin The Beguine. If the nuns had witnessed that, they would have died.

How were the nuns at St. Joseph's to know that dancing would be an issue? Boys never came in direct contact with girls until long after their care and teaching was over at St. Joseph's. Perhaps that was a good thing, for these Sisters of St. Joseph were a strange lot, I thought. An example in black and white sisterhood was Sister Mary Blanche, who fancied herself a technical teacher of the mechanics necessary to become a singer. An exercise used by her was to place the index finger and the thumb into the mouth and click the top and bottom rows of teeth with ringing fingernails that enabled the sound of tooth and nail. Click. Clack. This banging was designed to open the mouth wider and wider, creating a huge canal down the throat empowering the wind to escape into thin air and carry the sounds of angels ever higher and higher. She was a master at this exercise; unfortunately, her teeth took the brunt of the pounding and protruded at a 45 degree angle, almost pointing toward her cowardly students. She was a dynamic figure in black and white and seemed to sweat constantly. And yell, oh could she yell. She was loudest when she yanked up her long black sleeves and sang from the bottom of her being. Sister Mary Blanche yearned for similar devotion and effort from her students that never seemed to come, except perhaps from Colleen Nash. Colleen had a wonderful singing voice that the dullest of students recognized. Her reward was to perform at the religious functions that year as well as in the years to come.

At the end of the school year, everyone graduated from Sister Mary Blanche's grade five class, all with her well wishes for the future, plus her gift of a small three-by-five-inch framed print of the Sacred Heart that has been hanging in my home centred over the inside front doorway fifty years after my teeth escaped unscathed.

Going forward at the end of my sixteenth year was as foggy as Edgar Allan Poe's first glimpse of the House of Usher, but without the insufferable gloom. I saw nothing clearly; there was no apparent reason to quit everything I had known up to this point in my life and, to do it now. My family was supportive, but I was adamant. I knew that I wanted to get out of school and start to work. Was it money in my pocket, a car, or some freedom I thought a job would provide?

Was this why? The short answer is maybe. Hindsight reveals words like stupid and shallow, but whatever it was, I was resigned to doing just that. My mind knew something. My older brother Rich would equate intelligence with the pursuit of more intelligence through school and books—no one else on our street, no one who ever climbed the trees in the big yard, no one else in our entire neighbourhood went on to University but him. Everyone but Rich got a full-time permanent job around the ages of sixteen to eighteen.

Richard was sixteen months older than me and eleven months younger than Arch. Arch (1939) was the firstborn to Mom and Dad, followed by Rich (1940) and then me in 1941 and Joan in 1943 and Marilyn in 1945. Rich was the best student by far because he had the brains and the aptitude and drive to do well in school. Arch and Rich and I were altar boys in the church. Marilyn and Joan—being girls—were disallowed that privilege. That rule has since been changed along with meatless Fridays and many other dictates of the Roman Catholic faith in the last half-century. Arch and I were altar boys because it was the right thing to do, but Rich thrived in the rarified air of the sanctuary at St. Joseph's Catholic Church. Mom was very proud of us, she was proud of all of us. And when Rich grew up and took the vows of the priesthood, he was a distinguished and handsome figure of a man who had ducked several lovely young women who had their caps set on him. If those girls had turned his handsome and kind head, they would have had a great guy on their hands. Too bad Marie-Lou, Myrna and Gloria, I think you would have been good for him.

I have no idea how or why I developed the Puritanical Duty: "I shall not deserve anything unless I work relentlessly for it, with iron discipline, day after day." (Carlos Fuentes) I think I actually did inherit that principle or something resembling it, but it took a few years for the concept to grow within my spirit. I think my older brother had a hand in that, and I thank him for it. Rest in peace, Rich.

I was not 'popular' in the school sense of the word that kids seem to need. This yearning for popularity can permeate a person's thinking and actions. In many cases, this need can be a negative influence on personal growth. For me, I think I was more regular than popular in school or on the playing field. I have a 'Good Sportsmanship Trophy' that was given to me when I was eleven years of age by my hockey coach. The diminutive silvery memory adorns my mantle above the fireplace in the recreation room to his day. I was not the leading scorer, not the guy with the best shot or even a hard slap shot, but I was a good sport.

Chapter Two

I remember my early school days vividly and hope you will enjoy them. I enlisted *Alexander McPope* to help with this. You know who he is, don't you?

Adam Beck Atoms (1953)

On the corner of Dundas Street East (formerly Dole Avenue) and Greenwood Avenue stands a baseball diamond where the near greats played sandlot hardball. The little wannabe ball players in the late 40's had their idols that played for the "Stone Straws", and the "Bonitas." These were the big guys with complete uniforms and pinstripes adorning the grey or white uniform that indicated a home or away game, and the logo of the sponsoring company like The Stone Straw Company and the Bonita Theatre prominently displayed on their backs. He never knew any detail regarding The Stone Straw Company (other than they made drinking straws) that he could offer at the time of this tale, but the Bonita Theatre was well known to Gary and the rest of the neighbourhood as the "Show." Going to the Show was a big deal for him and his friends because an expense of 10 cents was the entry fee. But to play hardball, you needed only a team of eager kids who wanted to be like the big guys, and a coach like Barry Rule's old man who coached Adam Beck Playground, or the venerable Matty Eckler, a very big man who stood about five and a half feet tall who earned a living at the Pape Street Playground teaching kids to play games and compete, or the tall thin man with the red face who did the same job as Matty for the East Riverdale Playground; they called him Mr Flynn -- his teams were Pape's main competitor, along with Moss Park that was coached by Matty's old friend Gordie and Regent Park who never really had a permanent coach that he could recall.

Behind the ball diamond and the protecting screen was the place for viewing the game, you could barely see the ball leaving the hurler's hand and arriving in the catcher's mitt or cracking off the bat toward the berries in centre field, the pitchers were fast, and an important part of any successful team, but the hitters always gave them a run for their money. These games played by the guys in the nice uniforms were at night or Saturday afternoon -- and when they weren't playing for the large crowds that gathered there, the mighty Atoms would take over. Adam Beck Atoms consisted of his brother Arch behind the plate, his brother Rich on first base, Johnny Culliton (whose parents moved to Wellesley Street East at Parliament right in the middle of the season) at shortstop, his cousin Bill at second base, Eddy Noonan - whose childhood polio crippled his left hand, forcing his right hand to catch and throw immediately after removing the glove - in right field, Bruce Bracket was one of the Protestant kids in centre field or substitute catcher, when Arch went on the mound to relieve his brother Gary (Rubber Arm), who may have left third base to relieve the starting pitcher (Barry Rule) who always needed relief. Bruce Brackett's younger brother Allan rounded out the starting nine ball players, with Barry Rule's old man at the helm. They had substitutes that always got into the game -- winning or losing -- because that's the way it was.

Adam Beck Playground was named after a Canadian politician who founded the Hydro-Electric Power Commission of Ontario a hundred years ago. His name appears on a plaque by the ball field at Main and Gerrard Street East: the scene of some of the most notable slaughters of Adam Beck's young aspiring ball players, with most of it coming at the hands of East Riverdale and their incredible left-hander Marvin Berbeck. Marv had all the stuff that was needed to fan most of Adam Beck's hitters, while Mr Flynn's hitters chased the opposition pitchers out of the game on practically every occasion. Losing to those guys was tough to take; they seemed to have some kind of skill that was unfamiliar to their opponents. For example, Marv's old man had Marv pitch hardballs to him constantly when he wasn't working or watching his son pitch in a game, and while he did this, there was always constructive criticism that followed. Marv only got better, and he could mow the hitters down with precision with a mean fastball and a wicked off-speed pitch. Inside the other dugout, lurked a skinny kid with a pencil of an arm, and a curve ball that could move twice the width of the plate by the time it eventually reached its destination. His nickname was Rubber Arm, the protagonist of this story whose handle was aptly provided by his Uncle Allan one steamy hot afternoon looking onto the field, as he welcomed Gary to the pitcher's mound with a mighty, "Come on RubberArm." With that encouragement from a clearly home town fan, Gary proceeded to throw two wide swinging hooks that confounded the batter for a count of two strikes and no balls; and then the infamous High Hard One was offered up to the waiting slugger. Pitchers must have more than one pitch, if they didn't, most batters could get the hang of that pitch and ride it downtown when they could get the bat on the ball. They never touched the wide hook ever, but the need to develop another pitch, such as the High Hard One, was the downfall of an up-and-coming St. Louis Cardinal pitcher. He may have called it high and hard, but it really looked more like a beach ball to Flynn's kids, and they hit it for extra runs almost every time. Curses!

St. Joseph's Hockey Team (Peewee version, 1952)

Larry Brown, Jim Cowan and Hurricane O'Brien were the stars of the team; Gary's claim to longevity would be the silver cup that stands 6" high on his mantle in his recreation room. The cup is engraved "Good Sportsmanship Award" and is positioned 8 feet away from the other plaques commemorating the runner-up tennis champions of 1968 and other second-place finishes in squash, tennis and golf. That little trophy, the one with the good sportsmanship engraving, taught him the fundamentals of being a good loser and, if he ever got the opportunity, to be a good and gracious winner, someday.

The day, actually it was two days that came on a Saturday morning, they were two Saturday mornings back to back. The first being held in St. Catherines, a city well known for its young budding hockey players, and the second in the great Canadian city of Toronto. The St. Joseph Peewees had their equipment packed in several trucks waiting to be driven by several coaches and enthusiasts who had cheered them on to victory all season. They were on route to St. Catherines to play the first of the home and home series with the winners of the Niagara region's Catholic Youth Organization hockey championships (CYO) -- their team coached and led by Mr Corry's oldest son Bob was the overall winner of the Greater Toronto and district CYO. Bob was a good guy; he encouraged his charges to be the best that they could be at all times and in all ways. Their spirits were high as they weighed the evidence in their minds as to whose team would triumph, the very thought of a small-town team beating the likes of Hurricane O'Brien, Jim (the fiery Scot) Cowan and Larry Brown--the fastest and smoothest skater in the entire league--and Gary, who would soon to be receiving the "Good Sportsmanship Award" was unthinkable as the trucks rolled down Leslie Street to link to highway #2 and carry them westward to victory and their great reward. The excitement continued until the puck dropped at centre ice in their arena. Within a bunch of minutes, the St. Catherines team had scored five fast goals, and the visiting team had none. What was happening? This was a new experience for the team from the big city. Bob calmed them down when he said: "Hurricane, tighten up. Larry, turn on the jets. Jim, let's get busy. Everyone, listen up, we're not beaten yet, let's hustle, we can do it." They believed they could because the St. Joseph's peewees were the best in all of Toronto all winter.

St. Joseph's team began to look at their opposition's offence in a different light. The evidence and scrutiny yielded an observation that these guys were large, these guys were fast, their names were not names like Ted Kennedy or Turk Broda or Lionel Connacher, they were called Cullen and Hull and others unknown at the time. The game went on far too long; it gave their team time to get five more before the whistle blew, ending the misery of this road trip to the city of St. Catherines. On the way back to Toronto that night, Bob told his team that they just had an off night and that next Saturday at Maple Leaf Gardens, our team would give them a run for the trophy. He was optimistic and encouraging, if nothing else.

The next 6 nights passed quickly, and the following Saturday, all of the St. Joseph Peewees found their way to the greatest hockey shrine of them all: Maple Leaf Gardens standing majestically on the northwest corner of Church and Carleton. As you walk through the doors on Carleton Street, you see pictures of the Toronto Maple Leaf hockey stars adorning the walls, pictures of the Stanley Cup winning Toronto Maple Leaf teams speaking softly on the history of the great game to all who enter. The players--especially those that enter today--know that they have arrived when they hoist their hockey gear over their shoulders and march to the dressing room. The spectators would surely see a different game with a different result than the humiliation advanced in the Niagara district only a week ago; Bob Corry and his team would not be counted out in such a harsh and cruel manner; he would give the team the pep talk they needed before the biggest game of their entire hockey career and the only one Gary ever played at the Gardens. His parents, brothers, sisters, aunts and uncles, friends and foes were in the crowd waiting to witness the historic event.

At the point of skating on to the ice at Maple Leaf Gardens, the St. Joseph Peewees were ready for this game in every way. They had a healthy respect for the quality and ability of the team from St. Catherines as well as the confidence to give it their all, win or lose. There they were, dressed in the maroon and brown colours of St. Joseph's champion team, roaring on to the ice to the screams of appreciative fans from everywhere, and the game was soon underway. Larry was faster than he'd ever been. Hurricane was unbeatable in the net. Gary roamed the left wing and Jim stormed the entire ice surface looking for the opportunity to score. The fans went wild when the first goal was scored by St. Catherines. Bob Corry, momentarily at a loss for words, recaptured his enthusiasm and said, "You can score against these guys. I know you can." And he was right, after the allotted time for this rematch, the final score was 6 to 1 for them. The announcer had spoken the words, "Goal scored by St. Joseph's Jim Cowan--assist, Gary McDonald--time, nine minutes and fifteen seconds of the second period. This home and home championship series for the CYO's championship for all of Southern Ontario was won by a score of 16 to 1 by some of the greatest twelve-year-old players in the league. And one or two of these kids--unfortunately not Larry Brown, Jim Cowan, Hurricane O'Brien or Gary (good sportsmanship award recipient) McDonald--would, in another eight years, become household names in the big league: the National Hockey League.

Gary saw one of the best guys who ever laced on a pair of skates for St. Joseph's on June 2, 2003. A day that was 50 years later and Jim Cowan confirmed the outcome; that he was indeed the goal scorer and that Gary chalked up the assist. His wife Juta said courageously and with tongue in cheek that that was a defining moment in Jim's life. We know differently, don't we Jim?

As I write this, it saddens me to think the goal scorer mentioned above, my good friend Jim Cowan passed away very soon after we met that day. In several ways, we looked alike, especially when we wore the St. Joseph's Hockey Club sweaters and streaked toward the goal line, "He shoots, he scores!" I will never forget Jim and his 8 brothers and sisters who lived down the road from us. It was Jim who invited me to visit with his parents and all of their kids at their Bala, Muskoka cottage. It was there by the Torrance dock that life's new experiences for an ex-hockey player, ex-student of secondary schooling, and full-time printer began to unfold and turn this skinny kid into…well...who knows?

Chapter Three

Dad knew a fellow around the corner who was in the printing business, and Dad's logic was if I was not going to have a profession, with the only route to a profession through academic pursuits, that I should have a trade. So he told me to see Alf and ask him if there was a chance for me in his print shop. I met Alf on an evening in late August that year; Alf Barry was a cigar-smoking, red-nosed, rather corpulent and magnanimous recent widower whose career in printing spanned almost sixty years. The night we met, he said that he was getting out of the business now that he had reached the age of 70 because "there was no future in it." Alf laughed and I laughed with him; at what? I didn't know. In a couple of days, I had an interview with a Winston Churchill look-a-like named Andy, who was the big boss at Litho Print with an even bigger cigar than Alf smoked. I smoked in those days, as did the majority of our buddies, but never stogies. After an in-depth interview that lasted all of five minutes, Mr Kilgour put me to work in the shipping department of the company that I thought would employ me for the next 60 years.

Alf was the entire letterpress department and my new best older friend. Alf's department was located a few yards from the shipping department. Alf crashed numbers on bank cheques—a big part of the business that employed us. We also printed labels, cylinder covers for Gilbey's Black Label whiskey and one of my old favourite textbooks in Charlie King's Latin Class at Riverdale Collegiate: Living Latin.

[Please allow this slight digression to tell you that Charlie King was sixty-five years old and smaller in height than me; he taught at Riverdale his entire teaching career. As a group, my classmates were non-learners to put it bluntly. Mr King had an easy chair at the front of his classroom and he rocked it to and fro when he yelled at the dumbbells who faced him we heard statements like: "You darn

Hoolies, you'll never learn anything here; why don't you get out and get a job." I don't know what has become of my fellow students but I do know that Mr King retired at the end of my final year in High School. There would have been a cake and wonderful accolades from those who cherished his work at Riverdale Collegiate for 40 years.]

Mr King told me to go out and get a job. It was Charlie King's fault not mine.

[Please allow another slight digression to tell you that Charlie King used <u>Living Latin</u> at Riverdale Collegiate during his teaching career. His last year on this earth was unfortunately linked to the students in my class. He booked a trip that first summer of his retirement on The Queen Mary sailing for London England, tragically, unfairly and without warning Mr King died on board.]

From time to time, Alf and old Ken and I would eat lunch together while sitting on skids of paper. My mother always made my lunch consisting of two sandwiches, one was jam or peanut butter; the other was some kind of meat. Old Ken rattled his usual complaints about anything, including his lunch being the same every day. On one of those occasions I suggested he ask his wife to make him something else to make him happy. Old Ken looked at me out of the side of his whiskered face and said: "Wife? —I make them myself." He laughed, Alf laughed and I laughed, and this time I knew what I was laughing about. Soon Alf retired, we had another cake and a smallish party in Alf's one-man department and off he went to Los Angeles to live with his son. I saw Alf one more time after that; we met in 1965 in The Brown Derby on Santa Monica Boulevard in Los Angeles. He looked great, the cigar was larger than I had remembered and so was he. Alf had a little difficulty with his eyesight then, but he was living the good life in sunny California. We had a wonderful afternoon, and when I said goodbye to Alf, I knew that the time I spent with him was worth every hour of the four-day drive Knobby and I had endured with his girlfriend Lucy.

16

Lucy had relatives in California, and they had planned to stay with them, but on the way, the three of us stopped for a two-day visit in Las Vegas, Nevada. Big mistake. Eddy (that's Knobby's real name) lost his bankroll on the tables—he was stone-broke for the balance of the trip. I got lucky and met two lovely gamblers at a ten-cent roulette table who invited me to visit while I was in Hollywood. What they didn't say was that one of them was previously married to the sheriff. When he came in one Sunday afternoon to visit the kids, gun holstered to his hip, I vanished pronto.

Two weeks later, on the way back home, we tried Vegas again—still no luck. I've been back a few times since and it's always the same except for the ten-cent tables and the girls from Hollywood. Eddie and Lucy did marry and had three kids and a big life on Bay Street, buying and selling equities.

We returned from LA in the fall and after a year in the shipping department, I begged Andy to put me on a press to begin my apprenticeship. Andy had forgotten me while I was working with Scotty who wasn't a printer at all. He left the plant sharply at four o'clock every day with one of the bindery ladies. Filling shipping cases with deposit and withdrawal stubs all day long was less than I'd hoped for in my career. But I was patient. My patience afforded me the opportunity to meet one of the great charlatans of my life. That nameless reprobate was a frequent visitor to the shipping department as a transport truck driver. He showed up daily after four o'clock to pick up the predestined freight his company had been awarded by Scotty. On one of those days, he offered to sell his cherished and faithful 1949 Ford Custom for the princely sum of $300.00 and not a penny less. Yup, I bit and asked for a test drive. The following day the Green Machine showed up. I started this 'car' up and drove it around the block twice. Its operational characteristics seemed okay to me, and I trusted this bozo, so I bought it with $275.00 of my saved money and $25.00 I borrowed from Bruce Brackett and drove it home on a Friday night.

That evening I pulled into Nash's Texaco Garage and asked for one dollar's worth of gas. Mr Nash stuck his head under the hood and reappeared to apprise me of the current mechanical status of my purchase: "This car has no oil it whatsoever and I doubt if it has seen any lubrication in its ball joints for years." To him, I replied: "Please put the oil in it and give it a lube job." Mr Nash owned the local garage and his three sons worked with him. His was the only gas station around our neighbourhood. After Mr Nash and the boys did their work, I drove home around six o'clock with wisps of smoke coming through the floorboards and a wake of grey smelly smoke filling the air the length of Jones Avenue. The green-grey ghost was visible to all the neighbours, while the fresh grease caused the steering wheel to shake almost uncontrollably in my hands. I saw the S.O.B. that sold this wreck to me on Monday afternoon and I asked for my money back. He said that he would gladly take the car back except that he bought his kids some shoes and pants to go to school and that he was short of cash. In two months of embarrassment with the green, smoking, shaking monster of a vehicle I had it towed to the wreckers and they paid me $25.00 for the privilege. These wreckers—a great name for the boneyard of automobiles—were in the business of selling car parts and I was glad to be rid of the unsightly bottomless money pit once and for all. My education continued.

In due course (1958) Andy Kilgour gave me the job that he had promised, and I learned to love the hard work. My wrists and forearms became thicker and stronger from slugging sheets of paper as large as 52" wide and 77" long. Just so the reader has an idea, 500 sheets of ordinary coated paper at that size (4004 square inches per single sheet) weighs in the area of 320 pounds. No one person could handle that size of paper efficiently without kinking it. It took two of us working in unison to flop the stock and load or unload it. Vic Sluce was the boss of our three-man crew on the 77" Harris Press—he was also a member of the Whitby Dunlops. The Dunlops had represented Canada in the Olympic Hockey matches in the 1950's. I liked Vic and most of the other guys with whom I printed. Bob Massingham, a very cool

18

guy and a great golfer who worked in the stripping department, and Herb Forward who also slugged paper picked me up in front of my house and drove me to work every day when I was on the day shift (they never knew about the green monster; it was long gone by then). Ken Eldridge gave me the Lucas McCain handle that has stayed with me for most of my days in and out of print shops. After breathing and eating the spray of black ink at the delivery end of Vic's big press, Andy promoted me away to the feeding edge of a smaller press, where I met Ken.

The Lucas McCain nickname was Ken's way of drawing attention to a set of slightly bowed legs and my John Wayne impersonation. Into my third year with Vic, Ken, Jackson, Trotter, Nup, Boland, Bob, Herb and a very large group of very fine guys with whom I printed, with only fifty-seven more years to go and already a participant on the company hockey team, a frequent under-aged drinker at the company social functions, the king of wrist-wrestling matches with the boys on the street, the end came suddenly and without notice.

Andy Kilgour, incomplete without his huge cigar, his head hung just a little (I'm sure it was), fired me along with five others who may have thought they were lifers as well. We made room for the newest technology in commercial printing; they called it a web press.

Quitting was easy, but being fired was not—I arrived into the ranks of the unemployed at nineteen years of age, but not for long.

There is no creation without tradition. Tradition had us report to the union office and they had it all figured out this time. The union boss sent me to another company that hired me on the spot at fifteen dollars more per week over Litho Print's pay package. The other five guys went somewhere else, perhaps with the exception of Johnny Johnstone who was an older man and reaching retirement. Litho Print and the first crew of guys that I printed with will always be a meaningful memory for me. Once a month, I receive the union newsletter. The old names appear either as fifty or sixty-year pin recipients or as a one-line death notice. I saw Vic and Herb and numerous others, along with Art Hill's name, as a one-line entry over the passing years. They were all great guys and I'll never forget them. That 20% increase in pay was too easy, wasn't it? But perhaps it wasn't, because, now I was working all three shifts, one week on each and changing every Monday to another. The work was exciting and different, especially when we worked 7 days a week. This was new for me but I was young and the young should experience that kind of hard work, don't you think? The seventh day was the best when I arrived home at 8.00AM and returned to the ovens by 3.00PM to begin the afternoon shift for the next seven days. The ovens cooked and dried the sheets of metal decorated with fresh images and then trucked toward their destiny somewhere else in the huge, never cold, never stopped, never darkened plant in New Toronto we knew as Continental Can Limited, Plant 54. This was a goldmine for me—the overtime at time and a half or even double time on weekends was making me rich. I bought a brand new 1963 Corvair Convertible in the fall of 1962 for the unheard-of-sum of $3,500.00; it was all white with red leather seats and a black ragtop and I was on top of the world. Joan (my sister) and Garnet married that year and borrowed it for the weekend of their honeymoon. They looked great driving away with a few tin cans tied to the back bumper. I was proud of them and the car too.

Ross Cottrell was one of my co-workers at 'The Can' and he had one of these cars and swore by it—that is until I drove into the parking lot with mine. I pulled into a free parking spot next to good old Ross to hear him say: "You didn't buy that did you?" He thought he had a dud and never mentioned it until he saw mine. One of the stories Ross liked to tell was when asked by the foremen Walt McDavid why he wasn't at work last Tuesday, Ross was proud to tell his buddies that he responded with: "I came to work yesterday, but I couldn't find a parking spot in the lot, so I went home." And they never fired him! Weird? Perhaps you know about the General Motors experiment in rear engine vehicles—the Corvair was their answer to Volkswagen's incredible success with 'The Beetle.' Some of those Beetles and even a few Corvairs are still around today—but GM, along with the experience I had with mine knew it was a mistake of significant magnitude. My last day with the Corvair was in 1965 when the stupidly designed long fan belt that wound around its rear-mounted-gutless engine armed with two carburetors (can you imagine that?) flew off. My car began to slow down and actually caught fire. Handy loads of tossed snow and road dirt extinguished the oil pan fire while my passengers stood freezing on Lakeshore Road in downtown Toronto.

GM stopped making these cars a few years after I had licked my wounds again, saying to myself that someday I'll get a reliable car, but I think I'll take an expert with me when I put down my cash. The car I owned between the Green Machine and the White Corvair was a 1958 Pontiac Pathfinder. The Pontiac was purchased with the help of Elgin Blandford, the mechanic who lived next door, who always snickered, if not laughed out loud, when he saw and smelled the smoking green dragon on our street.

The job at Continental Can lasted three years in total, with an annual layoff during the winter. During the third winter, I took a temporary job at Arthurs Jones Lithographing (AJ) in the west end of Toronto. I had two other notable temporary jobs the previous two winters, one with Cape and Company, whose foreman fired me after forty-nine straight twelve-hour days because I asked for the extra ten cents an hour that the agreed-to union contract had stipulated: the princely sum of 49 days @ 12 hours each X 10 cents per hour = $58.80. The other was Bryant Press, where Russell, the lead pressman (and my boss), refused to work until 8:00 in the morning and then wash up, dress and prepare to go home. John Dunn, the big boss in the pressroom on the day shift, fired the three of us. We had no say in the matter of washing up and changing into our street clothes on company time. John's point had been made without fanfare or a second chance at abiding by his rule. Bryant Press was paying us for an eight-hour night and John's words were: "Please work the full eight hours or else." I'm sure John wanted the press running when the day shift arrived to take over which would have given the company another 3,000 impressions and possibly another 3,000 impressions when the afternoon shift took over if they left a running press. Russell was a mild, rather scholarly-looking left winger who was not going to be pushed around by anyone. I never heard anything more about Russell for the balance of my time in the printing business—he was another one of those guys who dictated my fate. I was a team member, but still I didn't like it..

While waiting for the recall to Continental Can in the spring of 1964, I printed on paper at Arthurs Jones. During that winter, a posture of rebellion was building within me; I was unhappy and wanted a change but the kind of change I wanted was unknown to me. When I learned that the union bosses working in the union office in downtown Toronto had turned down my former boss Walt McDavid's request that I be sent back to my metal decorating position at Continental Can, I was livid. I had no notification of that request of any kind. I felt that my working life was not my own to control, I was furious. How could these union people not respect the individual and report the request of a man who liked my work and who wanted me back? They simply didn't. It was more important to place another man into that position and leave me where I was.

Things had to change; by now, I knew that printing (the only kind I knew at the time) was not for me. After six years of shift work, two useless cars purchased using my judgment exclusively, one good one with the help of Elgin and very little social life outside of my time at Litho Print, and now, working at a job at Arthurs Jones for a foreman who was a crook, a cheat, a loud mouth and soon to be exposed for his lack of interest in the well being of AJ and its owners, I was moving on before he could dump me too. And it could have been Australia with my British tennis buddy Ken Clifton.

Ken came into my life while I enjoyed the game of tennis at the Kew Gardens Tennis Club. He was tall, slim and athletic, with a number of very attractive young women trailing behind him. Two of them were Gilda and Rosalee. Rosalee was after him big time, and Gilda was just looking for a hitting partner. Hugh Dow who worked in the Advertising business at Maclaren, came with Ken who was an Art Director at Foster Advertising. They joined Kew Gardens and I thoroughly enjoyed their company. We played plenty of tennis and drank lots of beer at the local Pub. Gilda and I enjoyed each others company on and off the courts. Rosalee was mad after Ken and called me at work one day and asked if I could help Ken see that she was really the only girl for him. What could I say to either of them? I never knew Ken's age, but he appeared around 30 years of age to me, and Rosalee (originally from Australia with vibrant red hair and sparkling eyes) was beautiful at whatever age she was. I never spoke to Ken about Rosalee's telephone call to me.

Over a beer one night, Ken told me that he had a great time in Canada for five years, but now he was moving on. He suggested that I join him and travel to Australia, where we'd live under the sun and play tennis all year round. I gave that some thought for a few days, and when we met at Kew, I told him thanks but no thanks. Ken was on a plane in no time. He may have had Rosalee with him? He was gone and Gilda and I hit tennis balls at Kew Gardens Tennis Club for years to come. Hugh Dow became an executive at MacLaren Advertising.

Chapter Four

In 1964, Duncan McGregor appeared seven years after I started my printing career. Duncan was a recent graduate of Ryerson Polytechnic School and the son of the co-owner Mr Reid McGregor. Duncan and I had met in the plant and became acquainted—he was in the sales department with his dad. On one of those coffee occasions, Dunc asked me if I would like to join him in sales. I tripped over my tongue and said, "Absolutely."

The interview that Duncan set up with his father lasted approximately twenty minutes. Time enough for Mr McGregor to know that I listened intently and communicated both verbally and with readable handwriting. That was all he needed. He asked me to come to work in the morning in a suit, shirt and tie. He would deal with his partner Mr Adams, and a replacement would be found to feed the 48" Harris Two Colour press.

In the morning, I spoke to Art Hill, my former lead pressman, who was a silver-haired wiry older man nicknamed the friendly silver fox. I told Art, while dressed in my only suit (blue, of course, with specially built pant legs to accommodate my John Wayne walking impression) that I was now in the sales department. I also asked him to leave my work clothes and shoes tucked into the corner and out of sight because I might be back. He said he would and wished me luck and good fortune in the new job. Art was a gentleman of the first order. (Ten years later) I was privileged to speak at Art's retirement party in the plant. To my regret, I never saw Art after that day—he had told me when we had worked together that the day he retired would be his very last day around printing machines Full Stop. We never saw Art again—anywhere, except in that inevitable one-line notice that appeared in the news-letter.

When Duncan McGregor offered me a position in the Sales Department of Arthurs Jones (AJ), I knew this was a door opening that could bring purpose to my working career. The first thing I realized was that I knew almost nothing about the process and procedure required to get the job done. I really believed that I didn't know what I didn't know. Therefore, learning was top of mind every day, every way about everything. I knew that I hadn't applied myself at school, and I also knew that my future was now in my court. This was what I had not experienced with unionized activity in the workplace. But now everything was on me, and that's where I wanted it.

I started reading books, as many as I could handle. The first was one given to me by Duncan: <u>How to Win Friends and Influence People</u> written by Dale Carnegie. Another was <u>The Greatest Salesman in The World</u> by Og Mandino, which I gave to myself. That was just a start, and a good start it was. The balance of my learning came from clients, suppliers, co-workers and Books, Books and more Books.

Almost every individual I approached with questions was happy to give me the secrets of their success in their part of the process. In time, and it took plenty of time for my confidence to grow and represent the qualified people who worked at AJ. But more importantly, my confidence came when I became the trusted professional my customers and prospects wanted to partner with. And with every success AJ enjoyed, our good name moved steadily towards our goal: To Be The Best Commercial Printing Company In Canada.

To begin this instalment of my career, I was told to accompany the departing salesman and visit the accounts and clients he had served. George was a former pressman at Arthurs Jones and a few years prior, had been handed the sales job now being offered to me. He enjoyed some success for a few years, and as I would find out in two months' time, had started another printing company with several other less than loyal employees at Arthurs Jones with whom I had known in passing. Apparently, they had been double dipping into the pot of clients that fed the employees and owners at Arthurs Jones. Aside from the horror show that would soon surface as a result of their nefarious activity, and in short notice as well, I began to realize that the entire process of printing, or better said, lithography was an enigma to me.

My clients and prospects knew more about the complete process of printing than I did. My fellow employees, especially the ones in art preparation, camera, pre-press film and plates, possessed the missing link in my printing education. From printing plates, images get planted on paper or metal, yes I knew something about that transfer, but how did words and pictures get on the plate? I had no idea. But in front of the best clients anyone could hope for, like Ortho and Fiberglas and several others, I was an eager kid who would find out and deliver the goods no matter what. Any latent antagonistic behaviour I had encouraged in myself beforehand, that is, prior to the blue suit transformation, had melted into a genuine appreciation for the craft that I needed to learn in its totality.

The customers and gifted production crew members at AJ would teach me, and in due course, George's very silent partners who were still working at Arthurs Jones and redirecting some of Arthurs Jones work to their nascent empire were fingered for the double-crossing employees that they in secret actually were. Incredulously, how could they have thought that their daytime employers would not soon learn of their infidelity? While the industry is a large one, the community of commercial sheet-fed printing is conspicuously close-knit; a competitor, supplier or good customer would soon spill the beans. When they did, five men, including two foremen, two pressmen, and one Chief Financial Officer, were fired with cause but never prosecuted. George had resigned weeks before Mr Adams and Mr McGregor fired the others. I suppose their crime, although unforgivable by the men who trusted them and paid their wages, would not have been as bad if they had not redirected some of Arthurs

Jones work while still on the payroll. But they did, and they should have resigned many weeks earlier. When I look back to those earliest days, I wonder in amazement how Mr Adams and Mr McGregor who had been saddled with these disloyal and dishonest employees, had the fortitude to carry on? And then I think of Bob Carter.

To be perfectly blunt, the craftsman that taught most of the printing skills at Arthurs Jones after Bill Adams and a few others permanently moved to their cottages, was a diminutive hard-nosed former lithographic pressman we loved: his name is Bob Carter. Bob was the brunt of short jokes. Everyone has heard them too many times, so I won't dwell on tallness or lack thereof except to say that whenever someone walked in the room saying, 'where is he' with their hand jutting out of a horizontal position from their armpit, everyone knew who they wanted.

Bob could take a joke, as well as deliver one however, his growing stature was not built on witty replies, or size; his authority spread like wildfire throughout AJ because of his skill sets, his aggressive good nature and explosive outbursts on occasion when he just couldn't accept negligence and incompetence. In addition, his ability to apologize when he hit the nasty button made him a big man in my eyes and others who had felt its sting. Through Bob and a few others trained by him, we provided knowledge to our employees, clients and creative designers. People benefitted from knowing and dealing with Bob Carter. Basically, anyone who took an interest in the process learned from him. I like to think that Bob was our pledge to the industry, and in so doing, our persona as a printer grew exponentially as our printing techniques and processes spread even unto our competition. We heard these words from a worthy competitor whose admiration was unbridled when he said to his people, "Try to be like AJ and its employees and we'll get our share of the work."

Growing companies endure and move on; AJ was no different. My thoughts about the company I would and wanted to invest in was something like this:

AJ had its birth in 1906 when Mr Arthurs started the company; Mr Jones joined in the 1920's and Mr Adams and Mr Reid McGregor purchased control in the 1950's; Mr Duncan McGregor, right out of Ryerson University joined in the early 1960s, and earned its presidency and ownership in 1976.

While the dollar amount of $28,000,000 annually may not seem like a significant amount, please consider that blocks of type and relevant photographs produced in any colour of ink on any manufactured paper stock, and finished in a variety of ways for every single individual project will limit an ability to create the volume possible in other production facilities. However, this characteristic of our business gave us the opportunity to create and establish superior techniques and craftspeople that, simply put, did it better than our competition. That is a saleable commodity - and one that was used and practised by every person who worked at AJ.

Hiring individuals who would learn and apply these practices followed; the addition of top quality printing and pre-press equipment from Heidelberg followed; the addition of a new modern 75,000 square foot manufacturing and office building built by Orlando in Mississauga followed in 1984; and most importantly our reputation as a trusted and quality supplier of important documents such as annual reports, advertising and various promotional materials surely followed.

The driving force behind all of this is, without doubt, Duncan McGregor the son of Reid McGregor, who had asked me if I would like to join the sales force in 1963. My life changed when I accepted the inquiry, and his father accepted me.

This company of people had optimal leadership not always found in many companies. Duncan McGregor had the guts to speak out on issues he deemed fair, smart and dedicated to his goal. During each day, decisions were made for and against, but the goal never changed: to be the trusted, quality supplier of important printed documents beyond repute. Year after year, example after example cemented that trust between our clients, prospects, suppliers and employees.

In 1986 Jannock Corporation who were big in bricks, steel and vinyl liked AJ within the communication industry and made an offer for 50% of AJ with an option for the other 50% in 1991. Duncan liked the opportunity to join a larger corporation and accepted their offer on behalf of his five partners. We were delighted and accepted the cash for half our shares.

During the next five years, the "MacAttack" kicked in and everything about our industry changed. Designers became typesetters; printers became commodity producers whose differentials could not easily be distinguished. With these changes, AJ's intrinsic value eroded somewhat and the intelligent decision was to accept the price and sell the balance of ownership to Jannock in 1991.

The next few years have no real significance other than Jannock waited for a buyer while AJ produced top-quality work, as always. Duncan recommended that I report to Jannock while the For Sale sign hung over AJ's head until 1994, when Leland Verner made an offer to buy.

Let me close by stating that the 'Hands on Control' that made this enterprise successful would never be the same without skilled executive, tradesman and qualified leaders in our industry calling the shots. The collective leadership that had built this great company would resign prior to 1998 under the circumstances that followed Mr Verner's vision and tutelage. Unfortunately for Arthurs Jones and its remaining employees, clients and suppliers, AJ closed its doors forever in 2001 after 95 years of service.

I think I know now that my brother was right, as was Mr Adams and Mr McGregor, along with Edgar Rice Burroughs' inspired quotation: "I print to escape...to escape poverty."

Avoiding poverty and its dreaded reality can foster principles as basic as the skills required to earn a living. The future, as unknown as it is for everyone, is ours to plan for. And for me, I had a principle in play that worked: "I shall not deserve anything unless I work relentlessly for it, with iron discipline, day after day." This is a direct quote from Carlos Fuentes in an autobiography of his. Am I ashamed to tell you the title of the piece from which this quotation is culled? It's called How I Started to Write and it's a fabulous read. Any similarity to my title is purely coincidental.

Chapter Five

"What was your greatest sales experience, Dad?"

On a rainy day in May following several weeks of procrastination, I remembered:

An early success was with my friend Charles Borg and his partner Paul on the printing of the Canadian Imperial Bank of Commerce's introduction to Chargex *[The forerunner to Visa, a successful financial instrument.]*

The sale to CIBC was in the vicinity of $30,000.00 in 1967: a huge amount of money and the largest project I had seen to date; it represented about twenty-five per cent of my total turnover for the year. The work was relatively simple by design but technically difficult to produce. Charles was an energetic, transplanted Hungarian without a shy bone in his body. When he believed in something, he sold it, and he sold hard. Together with his partner, we mapped out a plan that would get this baby delivered on time and on budget. All of us were over the top enjoying this initial success which was huge for Charles and me.

I celebrated the sale the night the order was confirmed with LW and a few drinks at a swanky joint in Toronto. LW was a beautiful girl that I knew just a little and was determined to know just a little more at the end of the night, but that's another story. Charles and I went on to do big things in our business; we also knew how to party, some of which were at a cottage in Halliburton that my buddies from grade school rented for years. Charles brought his girl friend, who fit in perfectly on those memorable, warm summer afternoons and nights.

Loyalty in business is something to seek and maintain with ferocious endeavour. It will make your business flourish; it creates more business with less effort. Charles and I were loyal. He was a man destined for a large footprint in Advertising Agency pursuits, especially Pharmaceuticals.

I recommended Charles Borg's first Pharmaceutical Client. In a short period of time, his firm was designing and buying the print requirements for this and several other Pharmaceutical Companies in the GTA. Unfortunately, I was asked to deal with his 'Print Buyer' whose requirements were quality, fastest delivery with the lowest price. Those mandates would not help my company meet its goals. I was looking for loyalty, trust and a friendly working environment to produce our very best work. That was not what I found with and in the new man. As a result, I saw less and less work from Charles and Associates—additionally, our payables from his company were long overdue. After several additional months, we finally got to zero, and I stopped calling on his company, but I did call Charles to tell him why. He was saddened to hear my story but was not going to change anything. They marched on without AJ and me. Unfortunately, Charles' company went down in another few years owing a lot of money to its other printers. But still, I thought Charles to be a great guy who should have faired better.

Another sales experience more of a retention nature, rather than a new client or project, was Arthurs Jones [in the 1980's] was doing tons of business with a major pharmaceutical company; one that I had been entrusted with when I began my sales experience in 1965. The yearly turnover for this client in 1989 was approaching $1,000,000.00, with a large percentage coming from one important product line.

They had many products, and we did most of the printing for them. We had worked with them and enjoyed a wonderful and trusted position as their main print supplier. As it happened, there was a relatively new purchasing manager placed in charge, and she advised me on the telephone (unbelievably so!) that she was placing the printing for a particular product with another company. I was in shock when she delivered this incredulous edict but managed to say without too much hesitation, "Don't do anything about this for thirty-five minutes. I'm coming right over," and I hung up instantly.

While driving across town, I maintained what might have been a shattered equanimity on any other day and attempted to plot my course of action. In thirty minutes, I was in her corner office. There were three of us there that afternoon at a rounded table, the lady, as well as her predecessor, who was a man that I had dealt with for twenty years, and me. I loved this man; he had spent his entire working career with the firm, he was someone that I respected and worked hard for. I believed that we had a successful past and had enjoyed mutual success from our collective efforts. In due course after a few pleasantries, the lady told me that she was not satisfied with the reporting that she had been given and that she had found some manner of our service and work to be substandard and was going to 'try out another company that had been after her business for some time.' Her reasoning, while not falling on deaf ears, and would be dealt with later, was not sound or well thought out and spurious at best.

I waited for my associate to add his position. I had always tried to be on his staff but not his payroll and waited for his thoughts. His first utterance was that this decision was hers to make and that if I wanted to make a counterproposal, they would listen attentively and consider it. I felt they needed an answer right there, and with that in mind, I told him how important our work had been to them and us, also that Arthurs Jones had solved many problems in the past (especially with this product) to the appreciation of their company and its people. I continued for several minutes, recalling success after success in serving their company since 1965. He nodded his agreement to our past performance that had actually begun in 1944 with Duncan's father, Reid McGregor.

Yanking this work and turning it over to an untested supplier was uncalled for, and I knew it. With that, I boldly or stupidly said, "If you take this part of the business away from us, then you'll need another supplier for the rest of it as well." After a few minutes of less-than-important added discussion and clearly nervous body language from the three of us created by the bombshell that I had dropped in our laps, we agreed to talk in the morning. I quickly left the building and drove home. The next morning I was in my office expecting a call by 10:00 AM. I had not spoken of this to anyone at Arthurs Jones nor would I think of telling anyone else until I had exhausted my attempt at keeping this valued business. The phone rang at precisely 8:30 AM; it was the gentleman who called, not the lady. The decision that he delivered with clarity and to my everlasting joy had been reversed; all of this business was staying with us. During the balance of my career, that moment had yielded an additional $15,000,000.00 in sales to this wonderful company whose dedication to both our companies' success was always in evidence; but just as important to my personal growth, this unforgettable happening gave me the confidence to fight for business I had justly earned, to know the difference between strength and weakness and when to act courageously. But was this my greatest sales experience? It ranks well up there.

This story is definitely not my greatest sales experience; it is almost a non-story but one I'm itching to reveal. We were doing a load of printing for the head office of a worldwide farm machinery manufacturer in the United States. When we were awarded a project, not every time, but when it was a major brochure for the Canadian market, I would fly to their office on an Air Canada jet and a little commuter plane for each way of the trip to pick up the art and photographs at the beginning of the project. After doing the work back at Arthurs Jones, making the distribution across Canada for the parent company as required, and occasionally, flying back to deliver first-off copies to do a little schmoozing with these truly professional people that I was fortunate to be serving.

One unhappy day however, I was told by my American contact that I would be dealing with a new man in the Canadian operation and not them any longer. An even unhappier day, was the day I met this unforgettable person.

His first words to me after the introductions in his office were, "I know that it's your job to screw my company, but it's my job to see that you don't." I held on to my chair like never before. The balance of that first meeting was a blur with one exception: he wore a short sleeve shirt and spent most of the time scratching both of his arms and talking rubbish. When I got back to my office (car phones were not widely used then), there was a call for me to call him back about an inquiry on a print project. He wanted a price; he wanted it in twenty minutes; we gave it to him; he called back in thirty minutes requesting a revision; he needed it in ten minutes; we gave it to him; he called back in thirty-five minutes with another revision request, and needed it in five minutes. You get the picture; I can see him scratching away even now.

After dealing with this enigma of a print buyer, his Canadian boss called and asked me what I thought of his employee. He was apologetic regarding his question but asked me to be blunt. [I sensed the apologetic part.] I then told him about our very first conversation and waited for his response before I continued. That was all I was allowed or needed to say because he ended our conversation with this comment, "The new man is history as of this moment, and if it means anything to you, your story is the most revealing of the ones I've encountered." This fellow must have been scratching around in some other areas to have his demise orchestrated so quickly. I never heard anything from the short man with short sleeves, the constant itch and the worst master/servant attitude I'd ever seen. I do hope that he learned from this experience; he was a young man.

Maybe it's the one about the Royal Bank of Canada and its mandate to have their Annual Report printed in Toronto. It was in 1983 when they decided that Toronto was the place their report would be designed and printed. Two wonderful people from the bank came to Toronto and interviewed several design firms for the project. After they picked the best one, recognized by many, they then looked about for the best printer. The design company recommended us, along with two other firms, as requested by the bank. This deal was going to be done, and it was my job, as well as Duncan McGregor's [now the president], to see that we made the sale. To get the job done effectively, knowing the past Montreal experiences as expressed by the bank representatives themselves, we promised any amount of chargeable overtime on any day of the week except Christmas morning between midnight and noon hour would be available to complete the task. After several meetings with the client and the designer and some pricing activity coupled with sampling and tests applicable to the desired result, the word came down that Arthurs Jones had won the day. We were thrilled with this windfall: approximately $750,000.00 in sales to add to our swollen order book. Our typed proposal were the words they needed to hear. These were not idle promises, every word was the truth, and every action was pointed at delivering the goods and delivering on time: 10.00 AM January 9, 1984, Montreal, Quebec.

This was a pivotal year and project for Arthurs Jones. On the strength of this and many other significant clients in hand, Duncan had decided to bite the bullet and build a new plant and office in Mississauga and move in September 1984. Every piece of printing equipment of any quality was employed to complete the Annual Report for The Royal Bank of Canada in our very old printing plant. We worked 24 hours a day and 7 days a week until I was on a plane with fourty hand-inspected copies for the brass in Montreal on delivery day. I arrived on the 19th floor of 1 Place Ville Marie at 9:30 AM with fourty individually inspected books; the truck arrived at 10:00 AM carrying seventy-five thousand pounds of the same beautifully designed Annual Report with matte black backgrounds and highly glossed full-colour photographs depicting the worldwide activity of the Royal

Bank of Canada. My two representatives from RBC loved the report and the service and thanked me with salient comments. After a wonderful meeting with my new friends in Montreal, I was in a cab toward the airport. When I returned to Toronto, I gave my partner Duncan, a big huge hug in front of the office staff. This was a magnificent accomplishment by the people in our company and we were proud of it. With confidence, we marched on with our seven-million-dollar plan to build a new plant and equip it with two big-time new presses from Heidelberg. What a summer that was in terms of juggling our operation, having no effective downtime, and orchestrating all departments toward moving to our magnificent new plant and office in Mississauga on September 1, 1984.

Nonchalantly, in October of 1984, the Royal Bank awarded the 1984 Annual Report to our major and worthy competitor who priced the work at "a sum equal to the cost of a new Cadillac less than us." We were shocked by this news and disappointed, of course, but we recovered and won it back the next year and held it for many years to come. All in all, a great sale that netted AJ in the neighbourhood of $5,000,000.00 over the next eight years. But is it the greatest?

You're probably wondering about my greatest sales experience, aren't you? Because I am finding it difficult to pick one which will satisfy the title I am writing under. It would be easier to simply change the title, wouldn't it? Perhaps something like "Sales Experiences That Changed My Life and Perhaps Others Too" would be a worthy revision?

However, at this time, AJ was the honoured printer involved with two of Canada's leading banks for the printing of their Annual Reports. It was TD and RBC's 1984 Annual Report. I am proud to have been in a position at Arthurs Jones in future years when we added BNS, BMO, and CIBC to TD and RBC and produced all five of our Largest Canadian Banks' Annual Reports. It's hard to speculate what our worthy competitors were thinking when the news leaked out.

37

Chapter Six

I have developed an ability to balance the work I do with people I enjoy spending time with. It's amazing how simple that process is if you have the right individuals to work and/or play with. Here are a few that come to mind:

These gentlemen contributed significantly to my years in the Printing Industry. We worked together and became friends. I've singled them out only because we talked and met for a drink and a bun in November 2018. Duncan McGregor and I have had lunch twice a year ever since our retirement in 1998. We visited The Masters Golf Tournament to celebrate his 70th birthday in 2010 with four additional friends, all of which was organized by Duncan's wife, Lynn.

[A. McPope wants to cut in with his thoughts on their trip:]

After several welcome emails from Lynn McGregor, five of Duncan McGregor's friends would be accompanying him to the Masters in celebration of his 70th birthday. The announcement of this event was made at Donalda GC during a lovely dinner celebrating Duncan's birthday, and so began an experience that my guy had been eager to have, and to have it with his partner and good friend for the last 48 years was the bonus.

When they arrived at the Cuscowilla Golf Resort, a very comfortable four-bedroom, four-bathroom golf cottage was waiting to receive Bruce, Jim, Gary and Dunc in one cottage, and John and Dave were in another of similar construct. The setting was perfect, and Augusta National was an hour away.

Day two and day four were spent on the grounds of the fabled Augusta National Golf Club, where the grass is perfect. The design is well-known, especially Amen Corner, made so by the Masters annual springtime broadcast. Arnold Palmer, Jack Nicklaus, Gary Player and Television brought golf to the masses then and are still passionately involved. Jack and Gary are the senior citizens of Augusta now, and they are revered above all others--and not only because the rest of the greats of yesteryear (Bobby Jones, Gene Sarazen, Ben Hogan, Arnold Palmer and others) are all putting out in the great beyond, but because the youth of golf owes them a great deal of gratitude; and they show it too.

Day three and day five allowed Duncan and his friends to demonstrate their golfing prowess at Cuscowilla as well as The Reynolds Plantation National Golf Club: both very fine tests of golf. This is what I would call a great birthday celebration.

Duncan is an avid active golfer and tennis player, and we have had many excellent friendly moments on our courts and golf courses. We made the time when we were fit and eager to play because it was important for both of us. Duncan was the catalyst that caused my shift in employment at Arthurs Jones from feeder to sales representative. Duncan's father, Reid McGregor, had been in the industry in sales all of his working life and co-owned the company with Mr Bill Adams, who was in charge of production. They made a good team, something I would find out in due course.

In the meeting that Duncan orchestrated for his father and me, Mr McGregor spoke about his company and sales activity. *[This bears repeating that he asked me a question that required a several-sentence response; following my answer, he asked me to write something on a piece of paper. He thought about my verbal and written replies momentarily and then asked me to come to the plant and office wearing a suit and tie the next morning.]* I had the job, and I was elated. However, when I think of those days, it was Duncan's approval that made it all happen.

The preceding paragraph is meant to set the stage for a career that flourished because of my good fortune in meeting numerous key individuals. These particular wonderful gentlemen and I met individually in November of 2018 when I reached out to them. They have their own stories of success, but this is mine, and I'd like to share some of these anecdotes with you.

Dean Grant and I met as a direct result of both of us doing business with Fiberglas Canada's Advertising and Marketing Manager, Grant McDiarmaid, in the early 1970's. Dean owned and ran a design company, and from time to time, we'd meet in Grant's office but mostly (I admit) when we were socializing on the golf course. That sounds terrible, but it wasn't. It just seemed like the right thing to do outside of business hours. The three of us loved our golf; Dean was at Islington; Grant was at Mississauga, and I was at Brampton. We'd have a home and home games and a few cold beers that quickly disappeared on those really hot days. Because of our mutual interest as well as the skills we could provide to each other, we were a good fit socially as well as professionally. The three of us did plenty of award-winning work while we improved our handicaps. Dean is married with two daughters and continues to live in Mississauga. He works just a little now and founded a system whereby he spends about six months in Scottsdale, Arizona, in his home at Troon Golf and Country Club, and the other six right here in Canada. He has qualified assistants working out of his office in Canada, while he does what he does best working out of Troon.

We met at the Brampton Golf Club for lunch with Dean saying we'll have "Two Cleansing Ales" please. I hadn't heard that phrase for twenty years. It was one of my signature calls after a day's golf. What a laugh we had, and then he pulled out another, "Give Me Fifteen Minutes of Solid Rock and Roll." When Dean, Grant, Herb Marshall and I met in Palm Springs for a little golf and relaxation in a local establishment with an entertainer who called out, "What would you like to hear?" I roared that line out for all to hear. Dean never forgot it. Our lunch was a plethora of laughs and reminiscing, especially during the second 'cleansing ale' when Dean asked me to come to Scottsdale with him and to give him an idea on how long I'd like to stay. I promised myself that I would.

The other Grant that put us together was Grant McDiarmaid, who arrived in Toronto from Vancouver fresh out of University. Grant landed the position of Advertising and Marketing Manager at Fiberglas Canada to replace a retiring gentleman of the first order: Mr Charlie Ness. Something that stuck with me for all of my working years came from Charlie who said this during one of our early meetings in 1965, "When you think of me and Fiberglas Canada, I want you to feel that you are on our staff, but not on our payroll." Boy, was that wonderful advice coming from a man I respected beyond repute.

One fine day when I was waiting to see Charlie Ness, he roared out of his office and said to his two secretaries, Miss Wood and Miss Steel, as he ran off to another meeting, "Take care of Mr McDonald. I'll be back in fifteen minutes." Miss Wood looked at me and said, "What do you want me to do?" I looked at her and said, "Just be yourself." (Which was beautiful.)

When Grant McDiarmaid took over, he picked up after Charlie and kept the ship afloat. He respected Charlie's associates in and outside of Fiberglas, and for me, it was business as usual, and more of it too. We became friends who played squash at our downtown squash club and golf clubs at Mississauga GC and Brampton GC as often as our schedules would allow. Grant married a young lady he had met at our Squash Club. His life was now complete.

Unfortunately, their marriage didn't make it, and a divorce was on the table. I spent plenty of time with Grant at that time, and after the paperwork was done, he accepted the inevitable and moved on. I am happy to write that his next wife was with him until his retirement many years later. In 1994 when my wife and I divorced, Grant was in my court and helped me adjust to single life once again. I had married the woman who said, "What do you want me to do?" After 25 years of marriage, we had two University-aged sons when she said to me, "I want to be myself again."

One of my favourite guys in my Arthurs Jones days was Ray Cassar. He ran a colour separation film house and I suggested he call on us and do some of our work. He did, and he did a great job for us too.

I had looked him up on LinkedIn and we typed a few messages back and forth including, "Let's have a few beers sometime." Ray and I met at Snug Harbour in Port Credit at noon on November 14, 2018, and had a fabulous time booting the old stories around our current anecdotes.

Ray enjoyed great success in his business and personal life. He came from Malta with his parents and siblings right after WW11 and settled in Toronto. One of his first jobs was at AJ as a helper on a big Harris press with a bronzer dispersing bronze dust on Rust Craft greeting cards. This dust would end up all over the place, including down Ray's throat and up his nose. I worked on that Harris press with the Bronzer for a little while when the regular helper was on vacation. At the end of my shift, I lit up like a Christmas Tree. An antidote for your ears, nose and throat was milk, and to drink plenty of it all day long. Ray had better ideas for his life's work, as did almost everyone who worked the Bronze Powder. That stuff and the silver stuff never dried; it went everywhere the wind took it.

Ray left AJ and we lost touch until I heard that Graphic Specialties was doing great work in its field. And there was Ray, the owner and brains behind the enterprise who would deliver for our people for a long time. Ray arrived at my retirement party with a gift-wrapped Great Big Bertha golf club which, at the time, was all the rage.

One of the great traditions at Brampton Golf Club is the Hole-In-One Club wherein once a year, each member who scores an ace is honoured by the non-scorers of that incredible shot at a banquet. The shooters are bagpiped into the room, sit at the head table and deliver their stories one after the other. They also receive a pile of money and an appropriate trophy for their personal wall of fame that may or may not exist in their home. My boss was one of those lucky guys. I wrote the speech for him, at his request, of course, and he delivered it to his buddies at the club. So here it is as I wrote it; who knows what he did with my words and studied syntax when he delivered it on November 1, 2013? Thank you for your patience friends; it's a tough job I have.

"When last we met like this....me here, you there....I told you about a Pro V1 golf ball, labelled with Brian Rennie's Adaptall logo, found in the bushes and gifted to me by Ernie Smith. When I teed it up and struck that ball with an old hybrid club purchased for twenty dollars out of a barrel in Florida, it found a perfect trail of freshly sown sand leading it right into the 16th hole on opening day 2008. A moment of great triumph, to be surely witnessed by Charlie Oxley, Ron Cote and Roy Heron.

This time I was teamed with Barry, Bill and Bob.....that would be Zeagman, Maxwell and Dool. We were on the tee at 12:30 when Dooley lurches from the lounge, rushes to his clubs and removes them from Ziggy's cart, proclaiming that he wanted to wait another twenty years for his second game with me. That said, the three of us tee off.

We manage a net-best ball of 3 under on the front nine and then catch fire with several net birdies, a net eagle and the net albatross on 13. My swing...with a newer Hybrid club and an almost new Pro V1...employing all 710 swing changes initiated last year and polished this year, produced a slight draw in the wind blowing from right to left and the perfect result. Binu—one of the golf pros—heard the roar from the 13th tee and left his 14th tee for a look into the hole and gave it a thumbs up. When we arrived at the hole, we had another round of hi-fives and Bruno told me to get working on the speech and I promised not to add too much bullshit like I did on the last occasion.

After the round, Barry, Bill, and I turn in our score of 13 under par, along with 30 dollars to Charlie Oxley, who is doing the math for Sandy Macintosh. Charlie also finds us a blind fourth...and of course....that turns out to be the inimitable Bob Dool. A moment of great triumph once again when I hand over Dooley's unearned-share of the loot.

It's not often that I have told you that my life has been made more complete by my association with the members and staff at the Brampton Golf Club. Traditions like the Hole in One Club with all of its history and entertaining speeches like Mondo's and Elliot's...remember those?... and many others is a tribute to all of you, and of course, those of us at this table who had the good luck to make a hole in one. Thank you for that too.

There is another tradition on the drawing board at our club, and if you allow... I'll give it just a little nudge. Amongst us are current, past active members who have improved our time here and made Brampton one of the best private clubs in Southern Ontario. They deserve our recognition in this newest Forum. So please dig into your personal memories and make your nomination one that counts. The first Brampton Hall of Fame Induction Ceremony will be a moment of great triumph for everyone. Thanks, guys...you're the best."

[In 2022, BGC holds its Inaugural Hall Of Fame Night. The honourees are Bob Little, Stu Hamilton and Pauline Kelly. It took a while, but it's done and a credit to those who made it happen.]

Chicken wings are savoury little treats. I have enjoyed these delicate appendages while my fingers dripped without restraint and hot sauce sloshed everywhere. But there is another kind of wing: the dreaded Chicken Wing that has plagued my golf swing to the point where I have decided that I will not ignore its consequence.

Why? Because for me, the game of golf demands continual improvement just for the hell of it, or better said, just for the fun of it. After being given the right instruction, I am currently attempting specific physical manoeuvres, applying patience, anti-inflammatory assistance and perseverance presently allowing me to think that eliminating the chicken wing just might be possible. And that I just might get the job done by the end of the 2010 golf season.

If you see me on the driving range with an old golf glove stuffed into my left armpit, which I'm supposed to hang on to under pain of death during the through-swing, please don't laugh too much: it's just one of a few quality tips I've been given by several very competent Golf Professionals at our Brampton Golf Club. If this works for me, I will put it in writing on my sixty-ninth birthday. If it doesn't, it was worth a try.

Yesterday (June 4, 2021), on the par three seventh hole at Brampton Golf Club, my five-wood shot stopped 6" away from a Hole-in-One that would have been my fourth of all time. I was playing with Ray Coole, Paul Hurley and Dave Hastie on our regular Friday game. Ray is eighty-nine years old, a past Ontario Amateur Champion who has been playing at our Brampton Golf Club for fifty-five years. We are a foursome who never keep score, play from the forward green tees and have a very nice time out there. There is plenty more on Ray Coole just below the next paragraph.

Mr Tak Tanaka was a regular, a gambler, an architect and one who designed some of our buildings and offered my son Rob a summer of employment in his firm before he left for U of T Architecture School. During one of our matches in the club championships, he called the head pro, Don Lunn, over and said, "Look at this guy chip and putt.

45

He's been doing that all day." Our match was very close, but Tak prevailed that day. He's been gone for a long time now. Don Elliot also passed away too early. Don was a fussy Englishman who admonished the waitresses when his glass of beer wasn't 1/32" from the very top of the glass. He was a great one for gimmes too -- it had to be within the leather of the grip or it was a no-go. Don was also the statistician who always kept the score and advised all of us how much we owed him, that was just before he took us for more money playing GIN. Bill McMahon had cancer. It was skin cancer and Bill would show up religiously wearing another bandage in another place every Wednesday on the first tee and go home long after the GIN game was over. There was another gentleman that had the same breakfast -- a half grapefruit and a bowl of oatmeal -- every day of his life, except for the time he enlisted with the RAF in England from 1939 to 1945. He was an avid golfer in a swashbuckling way. He liked to play, never practised but just got out there until he couldn't do it anymore. That was when he was 88 years old and said that was enough. He and his wife lived in a house that he built in Cheltenham, Ontario, until Jean said, "Roy, I can't do this anymore. We're moving to a senior citizen home in Brampton." I met the two of them at Greenway Senior's Home, where I had been convalescing for 18 months. And there he was in all his glory, absolutely hating the fact that he was not in charge in his own home. Roy didn't last very long at Greenway. He went downhill quickly and past away. Roy's best buddy was Ernie Smith who was a fair golfer with a temper. One time after a poor shot, his club-throwing skills missed me by about 36" on the par three 3rd Hole. Ernie was a great fisherman of lost golf balls and at Christmas time, all of us got a gift-wrapped bag of his best Titleist ProV1's. We heard that his basement at home was full of them. Ernie passed away six months before Roy. Ron Cote was my partner when I first joined in 1984. We had plenty of fun challenging a different twosome every Saturday. If we won the game, I had a small camera in my bag to take their photograph as one of our many 'conquests.' Ron and his wife Bernice were great friends and I called them often and socialized with his family: seven sons and daughters, twenty-five grandchildren and now the great-grandchildren are arriving. Ron left the Brampton Club ten years ago, Bernice left 2 years ago and they are still going strong at ninety years of age.

The Brampton Golf Club celebrated its 100th Anniversary 1921 - 2021. One of the stories being told is about my good friend Ray Coole. Here are some of Ray's thoughts as he recalls his 60 years at BGC, "It turned out to be a fantastic week. I was staying with relatives in Bowmanville and each morning I would wake up, eat breakfast, pack, and thank them for letting me stay. Because it was match play, I had no idea if I would be coming back to their home at the end of the day. It went on like that all week. It was a great run and showed me that I could compete against some of the best players of the day. It certainly gave me something to shoot for in future years."

This quotation was written by a Journalist on the occasion of Brampton GC's 100th Anniversary Celebration, "A year later, it was time to tee it up for a second shot in the Ontario Men's Amateur Championship at Highland CC. In battling his way to the title in 1957, Coole lived up to his last name with five of his seven matches going 18 holes. After two comparatively easy wins in the first and second rounds, he scored 1-up victories in the third and fourth rounds. His next two wins came over future Canadian Golf Hall of Fame members, a 2-up win over Gary Cowan of Kitchener, and then a 1-up victory against Nick Weslock of Windsor, the pre-tourney favourite."

These are Ray Coole's thoughts on his Amateur Champion wins in Ontario, "What I remember most about the victory were the three final matches that went right down to the wire when Bill Parkes, Cowan and Weslock all drove their tee shots on No. 18 out of bounds down the right side of the fairway," At the time, he was all square with Parkes and Weslock and 1-up on Cowan. Coole defeated Bill Morland of North Bay 1-up in the 18-hole final in a back-and-forth battle that he clinched with a par on No. 18 before about 1,200 spectators.

[Ray continued to play competitive golf, and over the years won twelve invitational tournaments across Ontario. He won the Brampton Men's Club Championship four times (1967, 1975, 1977 and 1978), twice in match play and twice in medal play. He also won the Brampton Senior Men's Championship twice (1986 and 1992).]

Ray was on the club's Board of Directors from 1968 to 1976 and was Club President in 1973. "I remember being involved in the hiring of John Henrick as our Head Golf Professional back in 1969. He was a touring pro at the time, and we had to make sure that he was prepared to settle in as our head pro and not continue to tour. I played a lot of golf with John over the years. He was a good friend," Ray says, noting John was at Brampton from 1969 to 1990 and died in March 2020.

I want to leave this story about my friend Ray of 35 years who said this about our Golf Club in 2021, "It is a terrific club. We have a really good course and so many great people. I really enjoy it here," [says Ray, who became a Legacy Member (85 years of age and 50 years membership) at Brampton in 2017.] "The Board of Directors have always worked hard to continually make improvements to the course and the clubhouse, so members enjoy their time at the club. It continues to get better, and I am looking forward to the club's 100th anniversary this year. It is hard to believe that I have been part of it for nearly 60 years."

And Yours Truly has been playing golf with Ray for 35 years. We are currently in the Trackman Simulator at BGC on Winter's Monday mornings at 11:00 honing our swing, possibly buying the latest technology that promises lower scores yielding more fun than you can imagine. Ray is a gentleman of the first order, and I can't wait for our next Friday game with Ray, Paul and Dave.

It was at Brampton GC where I met Ron Wicks, a former National Hockey League Referee. Ron's claim to fame was as a referee, and not a golfer. He had a slap shot of a golf swing with magnets taped to most of his body. These bits of metal were intended to ease the pain of muscle and bone that had served him well, but now, all of it just hurt.

Alexander McPope wants his voice to tell you this:

During Gary's time at the Brampton Golf Club and YMCA, he has met several accomplished individuals, not the least of these is Ron Wicks of the National Hockey League - the very big league that spawned the likes of Punch Imlach of the once, oh so long ago, mighty Toronto Maple Leafs. In his book, Ron reveals that Punch called Frank Mahovlich 'Mahallovich' just to get his goat; that Bobby Orr was his choice as the best player he'd ever seen play; that Alan Eagleson for whom Carl Brewer said, "Thank God for the United States of America" when The Eagle was found guilty of stealing money from the very players he was paid to represent; and the World Hockey Association where players and referees were offered employment for FIVE times what they had been getting in the NHL; and hundreds of other colourful anecdotes and constructive criticisms that, if implemented, would leave his profession a better place. And when it's all said (and of course printed), most of us want to be remembered long after the post-mortem. So this is where I come in...

Ron Wicks begins his book with, "For more than twenty-five years, I loved my job as an NHL referee. Moreover, the twenty-odd after-years of being involved with benefit hockey games, golf tournaments, and the like are every bit as interesting. So interesting, in fact, that a former colleague and several of those players that I personally tossed into the penalty box have encouraged this moment by saying to me, "Why don't you write a book?"

Along with many of Ron's friends and my boss Gary, who is apparently named 'Buzz' from time to time, I would like to wish Ron and his book A Referee's Life all the success that it richly deserves. You can purchase this 140-page book for the princely sum of $19.95.

It's at General Store Publishing House, 499 O'Brien Road, Box 415, Renfrew, Ontario, Canada K7V 4A6. Telephone 1 800 465 6072 http://www.gsph.com

It has been a pleasure to serve but I must add that Ron Wicks passed away a number of years ago. I have my copy of his book.

Sincerely and Respectfully,

Alexander McPope

Chapter Seven

When I retired in 1998, I took a trip to Wimbledon with Kathy Jarvis who had introduced me to the game of tennis in 1961, and quickly at that time destroyed me on her court at Kew Gardens Tennis Club. Kew is a public facility consisting of ten hard courts at The Beach in Toronto's East End. We were twenty-one years of age when Kathy challenged me to a game of tennis right after I licked my lips over a Dry Gin Martini poured for me at her family home. Kathy lived about 200 yards north of me on Sprout Avenue from the time we were born. We went to St. Joseph's school and church. After the second Martini, she asked me to have a game of tennis with her tomorrow morning. I said, "Tennis? That's a girl's game." We talked some more, drank some more, agreed to meet at Kew and then I left.

In the morning, I wore white shorts, a T-shirt, running shoes and arrived at the Kew Gardens Tennis club to meet Kathy who introduced me to Mrs Davis who learned that we were friends and blah blah blah. Mrs Davis knew that Kathy and I had a bet as she winked and escorted us to court number 10, away from the 'pomp and ceremony' surrounding the scheduling board that Mrs Davis had managed forever. When our half hour was done, I couldn't believe how badly I was beaten. I went directly to Mrs Davis and admitted a total inability to actually make contact with the ball and asked how I would go about learning this 'girl's game.' Mrs Davis asked for a $15.00 annual membership fee and said, "We are here from day break seven days a week, and are happy to have you join the club."

I spent the next 25 years playing tennis developing bad knees and winning second-place finishes except for two lonely winner's trophies: one for mixed doubles with Anna, and the other was the B Flight Men's championship.

I learned to love the game and think of the fun times we had Kathy. Whenever I hear the name Wimbledon I think of you.. Thank you.

Balmy Beach Canoe Club 1903 - and still going

An early introduction would have been in 1958 when the Litho Print hockey team participated in an event with a Saturday night dinner and dance. I went without a wife or a date, and I had neither in those days. Nup, Sluce, Boland, Eldridge and others were the senior guys at the plant who had invited me to play on the team. I played one game on a Sunday morning somewhere against some other team whose name never found its place in my memory. The drink at the Balmy Beach club was flowing even to me who was under the legal age. Those were memorable days with the first group of printers I knew. There would be several other firms that employed me, some for a very short time, and one for a very long time.

In 1963 Geza Zabados, a terrific tennis player from Kew Gardens tennis club asked me if I knew anything about his wintertime racquet game called Squash. I had no knowledge of it when he introduced me to Balmy Beach and a game that would occupy my winter sporting life. (The first time I played this game, I was seeing black spots before my eyes.) But I loved the game and played it with passion until the required wrist snap was no more (the spots had disappeared years ago). Additionally, squash cultivated many good friends for me now that we lived in 'The Beaches.'

Thirty-three years later (2019) on a failed trip to St. Lawrence Market during a crisp and sunny afternoon, we ended up on Scarborough Beach Blvd. to have a look at the old home and take a few photos. We never expected to see any of our neighbours, but we did with Mark and Ruth Lerner who still live two doors north. I then had the bright idea to have a drink at Balmy Beach CC, a member-only establishment since the 1920's. Terryl and I introduced ourselves to the barkeep manager, and she poured us a drink where the nostalgia appeared on every wall and cranny of this old, old building. They were

52

still there: Glen, Bart, Alex, Bob, Rob and others standing around a large circular table having a beer and talking up a storm. It was as if time stood still. These guys were still playing squash; I saw Glen and Bart hammering that little ball tight to the wall. Upstairs was the plaque on the wall - Geza's name is on it - with past champions in full view. Ken Lane, Peter Jacobson and Craig Wells are memorialized over the courts in two-foot-high letters. The war painted canoe paddles hang over the fireplace and team pictures are everywhere. Nothing has changed except for a coat of paint here and there just as I hoped.

CCCottage Reunion Sept 14 - 21, 2019 Saskatoon, Saskatchewan

I'm booked and checked-in on Air Canada's #1123 at 11:00 on September 14 arriving at 12:33 to begin our 20th reunion since John Delisle convened the first one in 1995. Many a tale has been told and retold since the mid-1960s when it all started in a small cottage as our weekend retreat. I think there were 12 guys who formed the original group, with Arch, Bill and me signing on for life a couple of years later. (We were the old guys who were allowed to hang out when some of the younger decided their weekend-time would be better spent elsewhere.) That roster remains to this day except for Pat and Arch who passed away rather suddenly. Jack, Phil and Paul have been replaced by Rod, Eric and the odd mystery guest (one named Piggy comes to mind) whose sudden appearance illuminates our gatherings from time to time. Our yearly experience seems to stay ignited by regular emails about horse races, football pools, birthdays, trips to the hospital and other remembrances of special occasions like anniversaries and a whole lot of times that make up the constant mix of our lives.

I've told our story to friends and, to a man or woman, they marvel at what we have been able to achieve and maintain for fifty-four years. Oh yes, the 'CCCottage' was uttered by cousin Bill who stuttered a great deal as a youngster, but now reaching for 80 years his voice's ability has improved considerably.

On September 14, 2019 Ted, Tom, Bill, Dan, John, Mike, Larry, Rod and I arrived from various places across Canada to give and receive generous man hugs all around; and then pile into cars and set off for Emma Lake—about a two hour drive north of Saskatoon deep into a land of many lakes and wild life. We passed Elk and Deer and Coyotes before settling into a very nice cottage donated by a friend of Ted's at zero cost to us. The food and drink had been purchased on Friday; the fishing and golf equipment was stored in three SUV's. Dinner was prepared, eaten and cleared away for the poker game to follow. The rooms had been assigned and the older guys got their pick, and why not? That evening I was awarded the "Gary McDonald Come back Award" as its first recipient. Mike Bird was the 2nd.

The week was full of poker, golf, fishing and stories of our good old days in Southern Ontario and ended on the beach with a huge fire and fish fry. How sweet it is.

Cabin Fever Calendar 2005

The evening was full of Air Canada employees who often find a way to get together and talk about their lives in and outside of their work. December 7, 2004 was no exception. There was a steady level of human behaviour with all the lively body language and talk that brought the room to life. Of course, there were drinks and hors d'oeuvres prior to and throughout the party intended to launch a very slick and carefully planned product benefitting Canada's leading hospital for the treatment of cancer.

Cabin Fever Calendar girls are flight attendants who are fun and fabulous women. I know this to be true; Gary is pictured in the September shot with Terryl and he asked me to create this page; and then he had the nerve to say he was a consultant! Here's the proof: they spoke at the Launch Event at the Indian Motorcycle Club in Toronto on December 7, 2004.

Speech at the Indian Motorcycle Club during the Launch of Terryl's Air Canada F/A Cabin Fever Calendar.

"Here is one fabulous fiftyish girl partially revealed on the September page: her name is Terryl Smith...I call her Pud! I'm speaking tonight only because Terry lost her voice doing the tango with me in Argentina last Tuesday. If she could talk tonight, I think she would speak to you about Sisterhood and Support. In her view this mini infrastructure is at the heart of being a flight attendant. I don't know why that is so, but it is. I've seen that sisterhood first hand: When they see their sisters at 39,000 feet ...or at sea level... they are friends...they are family doing a fairly stressful job oft times under difficult conditions...which leads me to the support I see when the tough times hit...and it does because they're human too. Their support for one another is never more evident than when one of them has been hit with Cancer. Magically a flurry of telephone calls and emails organize things like meals for the kids at home...donations for the wig that will be needed in due course...rotating regular visits to their homes and life-saving places like The Princess Margaret Hospital. In short… these women bring plenty to the table when one of their own needs a hand… or a shoulder to cry on. There are around five thousand flying angels in Canada. There are 14 of them posing in this calendar with many more contributing their time, energy and goodwill to bring about the 2005 Cabin Fever Calendar being launched here tonight…they did this for the Princess Margaret Hospital…they did this for their sisters…and for everyone who may need that special help someday. Terryl wants me to mention the intense effort made by the entire committee, especially Ruth Fotheringham and Kay Woolam whose altruistic efforts should…with your help… garner a cool 100 Grand for the Princess Margaret Hospital. She appreciates and acknowledges the media here tonight especially Ted Woloshym of CFRB…they will get this project off the ground and in the air… in a manner of speaking. Oh…. Terryl does want to try to say something…. Go ahead Pud":

Terryl did speak with great difficulty but also with important words for the people who gave their time and slightly undressed selves to bring this event to life. She also asked for their additional work to sell these Calendars for $10.00 each to as many friends, associates and complete strangers as well. In time their target was oversold and $125,000.00 was donated to the Princess Margaret Hospital, whose work is so important to all of us.

Terryl is a very important person to me. From time to time in conversation, I mention that Terryl received the highest commendation that Air Canada gives which is: The Award of Excellence. It also seems to me that she is embarrassed when this is brought up. But, I would be remiss if I did not include her wonderful achievement in this memoir.

Chapter Eight

Travels with Terryl

W hen Terryl was very young and the urge to be someplace else was upon her, she acted boldly and signed on with Air Canada, and, as it turned out for her, the itch continued. I never knew that that itch would affect me when we met in October of 1998. But it did—eventually, but still not to the degree that commands her daily thoughts. Why just the other day when touching down at Pearson Airport in Toronto Terryl took my arm and said: "Where are we going next?" I laughed and chuckled about that and only ten days later I was asking myself that same question.

This chapter will recall someplace other than where I live or work, not only as Terryl's accomplice on layovers around the world and not only on vacations of which there have been many: I will recall trips to the United States and Europe and record these experiences as having a major influence on me; but mostly on what and how I think about the world and its people.

We have been to London, Los Angeles, Lima, Las Vegas, Munich, Madrid, Melbourne, Paris, Frankfurt, Glasgow, Dublin, Rome, Tokyo, Trois Riviere, Sydney, Saltzburg, San Francisco, Shawinigan, Santorini, Shanghai, Santiago, Saint John, Saint Johns, Auckland, Christchurch, Cairo, Calgary, Athens, Alexandria, Amsterdam, Bogotá, Buenos Aries, Antarctic Continent, Valparaiso, Hobart, New York, Honolulu, Istanbul, Limasol, Venice, Victoria, Vancouver, Edmonton, Winnipeg, Montreal, Quebec City, Halifax, Bala, Beijing, and yadayadayada…and back again; so where to next should not be a problem: Stockholm Sweden and St. Petersburg Russia are on the radar. If I take these names separately, there is a story to be told about every place, and more importantly, a story about the people we have met and the lives they live, all wonderfully different and unique for sure.

Traveling has never been a source of great excitement accompanied by careful, fastidious plans orchestrated to meet grand expectations. No, it's a matter of getting somewhere else, perhaps it's a place I need to be or a place someone else wants or needs to be. There is a difference. And in that difference planning and expectations differ. Mine for example starts with packing. My former wife packed my stuff when I was going on a trip. But one day I suggested that I did not need a particular item, but did need another item. On receipt of those words she stopped packing my kit forever. I rather like packing my own stuff and need to be alone, a selfish act that allows me time to concentrate. Are we the same when it comes to packing?

The best way to get from place to place, especially if it takes more than seven hours to drive, is to fly, and flying with Terryl is a total joy for me. Her time at Air Canada has its perquisites, and not the least of these is the lifetime standby transportation that AC gives its employees and retirees. I'm not at liberty to provide additional detail—it's a trade secret, a secret that is known at my club where during winter months I hear these words too often, "Is Air Canada bankrupt? What are you doing hanging around here?" I sometimes reply that I need to come home to count the money I am saving.

This narrative is not about cost; it's about the experience, the experience of travel and seeing the difference that exists among places and people. It's about attaining a comfort level with unfamiliar habits practiced by unfamiliar people in unfamiliar places. If there is anything that scares some people off traveling it's the strange places, foods, transportation and even uncertainty that takes over. The way I have overcome these human traits is to say to myself, "Just do it." And in so doing, I have had food poisoning, bug bites, and been lost all over the place, but I have never been uncertain about the outcome: that we'd arrive in time to continue the journey some how. Running out of gas in New Zealand wherein we foolishly left a very nice little town looking for a thermal gusher that was off the beaten track without checking the gas tank's readiness to proceed was one of those moments. We had a map but it was one of the maps that showed us only the main roads; and we were a long way in a strange place looking for this magic steam coming from the centre of the earth. We had no compass, no GPS and no gas to speak of. My friend Jim was in charge of the car, and of course, we stopped at every house to ask for directions. Every house but the last one was empty of people--and the sheep were not talking our language. We were running on fumes when we were provided with a direction that pointed us toward the highway and a nearby gas station, a pump that we drove right on by several hours earlier. Who knew? These people are the Maori people (pronounced moldy) who are native to New Zealand. In this country, the Maori appear to be getting their land back from the government of the day. But it was one night earlier when we visited a tribal ritual whereby the natives greeted us with a feast and a greeting that I'll never forget. The natives appeared in the costume, of course…ranting, yelling and looking ferocious.

There is more to write about than just the rude awakening that pickpockets leave nestled in your grey matter; but I'm not in the mood for that:

Terryl and I visited Mazatlan again early in November 2010 because we had agreed to meet Charlie and Maureen Oxley in Puerto Vallarta on November 27. They have a couple of timeshare facilities and offered one to us at no cost for a week. Charlie and Maureen are good friends from the Brampton Golf Club; so off we went with our clubs et al.

During the time in Mazatlan, Terryl expressed an idea that had a great deal of merit, and that was to ask the older members of my family to come to Mazatlan with us in January 2011. We talked to our good friends Tom and Connie Deadman who had introduced Mazatlan to us even before they lived in a magnificent Penthouse overlooking the Pacific Ocean. Terryl's friend Joanne and brother Johnny Horsely and his wife Linda had welcomed us to many of their social gatherings. The Tequila was everywhere.

<u>Our Trip to Magicland</u>

During a just mentioned visit to a favourite destination in Mexico, Terryl, enthralled with the weather and the accommodation we were enjoying, went on record stating that my mom, two sisters Joan and Marilyn, two brothers-in-law Garnet and Buster, one brother Archie and the two of us would absolutely love a vacation together in the city of Mazatlan Mexico. I thought it was a great idea.

We emailed each of them, and in a few days, the replies landed: "Let's do it." We began making the arrangements.

Our collective planning had to include others who could take care of important responsibilities back home. (One sister cares for her grandchildren and the other cares for Mom, who turned 95 years old last summer.) The rest of us are completely retired with no responsibilities. Because Mom was coming with us there was no problem there—and the grandchildren would be looked after by their father and his brother-in-law, all initiated by one of mom's granddaughters who absolutely insisted that her mom and dad do this once-in-a-lifetime trip. (All of mom's kids would be with her on vacation, perhaps for the last time.)

I booked our flights and arranged for a ground-floor condo on the ocean, complete with an indoor/outdoor swimming pool, fitness facility and Palapa staffed with lovely people who enjoy their work. Two of us flew out of Buffalo, New York, with the other six on Air Canada from Toronto on December 28. Everyone arrived on time in Mazatlan (Magicland to our globe-trotting 95-year-old mom).

After six days in the sun with plenty of sightseeing and meeting friends in beautiful surroundings the focus of our intent changed overnight. Mom was starting to cough and was cold all over. That night, during another party in our condo, we called a Doctor to come and have a look at mom. Dr Arturo Cardenas arrived at ten the next morning, and in twenty minutes, Mom and my younger sister Marilyn were en route to the hospital in his car. They both had pneumonia.

For 95 years, Emma has truly loved people; she shows that love by being generous with her time and attention to people's needs and problems; she shows that love with her faithful smile; and she shows that love with laughter and a love of life no matter what! Now with each of us at her side, we saw all of those qualities in full flight even as she gasped for breath.

Dr Arturo seemed to be available 24 hours a day; he brought in his comrades who were experts in heart and respiratory problems and treated her with all of their might and skill. The nurses, save one, couldn't speak English; and even if they could, Mom probably couldn't hear what they were saying. (Her hearing has been disintegrating for twenty years.) My sister Joan spoke to her and told Mom that she would be staying with her in her hospital room— another smile filled her face, a face that seemed to be getting smaller and smaller under her life-giving oxygen mask. Mom couldn't get comfortable in that hospital bed; she tried and tried without complaining to the staff. Joan knew this, of course, and asked for an overstuffed armchair to be brought into the room. The attendants did that without question. The night passed and Mom grew weaker and weaker as the days turned into nights. Dr Arturo and his associates worked tirelessly to help but nothing seemed to work—and still, Mom smiled and thanked all of them for being so kind to her. After seven days, Mom was taken to the ICU wing where the seven of us were allowed in to see her one at a time and once a day between 6:30 and 7:00pm instead of all day and anytime. While I was with her, tears streamed down my cheeks and fell on her weakened little body, a body and soul that only thirteen days ago had been in full flight on vacation with all of her sons and daughters. It was at that moment that she said to me, "I love you and take care of yourself and Terryl; she is a wonderful girl. I just might be on my way to see your dad and Richard." When my time was up, I kissed her and asked her to find the strength to fight for survival. She smiled again and said she would try very hard. That night a complete stranger approached me in the parking lot of the hospital and pointed to his heart. I knew what he was saying.

Mom fought her way out of the ICU after five very difficult days, but back in her hospital room where Joan or Marilyn had spent every night except that last one, Mom was depressed, perhaps for the first time in her life. When Dr Arturo saw her, he told her that she couldn't go home until he saw that smile, the same smile that couched her expression of thanks that he and so many of his staff had seen and heard so many times during the twelve days Mom was in their care.

There it was: her smile was back the next morning. Dr Arturo drove her back to our condo with instructions for her care until we could safely return to Canada.

The sun shone brightly for the next six days; we bundled Mom up and put her in the direct sunlight with protective sunglasses and a monstrous hat; we wheeled her out to the pool in her own wheel chair, and the neighbours came by to greet her and ask about her condition. She smiled and said that life is a beautiful thing.

Mom is home now and in her favourite pink chair in her beautiful pink bedroom in Joan and Garnet's house. I know that she is smiling and training her magnifying glass on her pictures of our trip to Magicland and possibly saying, "This might be the last holiday when we were all together."

I hoped not. But it was.

Alexander McPope wants to jump in here to write about our trip to Russia

(April 10, 2011) Gogol, Chekhov and Tolstoy will be happy that my leader will finally be amongst them: the spirit of them at the very least during a portion of this cruise out of and back to Stockholm. You may not already know that this visit has been on his radar for a long time. Why, you may ask? His answer to that question should bubble up to these pages prior to the trip itself; and if it doesn't, then it will surely be written right after the event itself.

Did you know that The City of Saint Petersburg (founded in 1703) was renamed in 1914 and known as Petrograd; not to be outdone, in 1924, its name was changed to Leningrad, and then, back to Saint Petersburg in 1991? The politics of this part of the world is a moving target, so should its city's names, don't you think? Saint Petersburg is the most northerly city on Earth with a population of more than a million souls. I'm thinking about Nikolai Gogol and his Dead Souls, published in 1841, that established him as the greatest Russian prose writer who regularly lampooned the unseemly sides of Imperial Russia. I think his best work was The Overcoat. It's a story about an introverted clerk who suddenly becomes the toast of the town when he replaces his threadbare winter coat with a much-needed new one. Gary and I think you will enjoy some of his literature. The legend of Nikolai Gogol was something that Joseph Stalin was determined to suppress, and he did so in 1952 by taking down a statue of Nikolai and replacing it with something containing more of Stalin's version of Social Realism. Here's something by Gogol in Dead Souls that Nikolai was to refute in later years "...But there are passions which are not of man's choosing. For they are born with him when he comes into the world, and he is not given the strength to reject them. They are directed by some higher design, and there is in them something eternally beckoning, something which never falls silent all the days of his life..."

More to come, dear reader:

So he starts by talking about Alexander Pushkin (1799 - 1837), one of Russia's favourite poets, loved by the people and bronzed in front of Catherine's Palace in a town formerly called Tsarskoe Selo renamed Pushkin in 1937. *[The Russians love changing names, and he mentioned it to me a few times.]* Here is a piece of Pushkin's work:

'The Bronze Horseman'

"There, by the billows desolate, / He stood, with mighty thoughts elate, / And gazed; but in the distance only / A sorry skiff on the broad spate / Of Neva drifted seaward, lonely. / The moss-grown miry banks with rare / Hovels were dotted here and there / Where wretched Finns for shelter crowded; / The murmuring woodlands had no share / Of sunshine, all in mist beshrouded."

And thus He mused: "From here, indeed Shall we strike terror in the Swede? And here a city by our labor Founded, shall gall our haughty neighbour; "Here cut"--so Nature gives command-- Your window through on Europe; stand Firm-footed by the sea, unchanging! 'Ay, ships of every flag shall come By waters they had never swum, And we shall revel, freely ranging.

[I'm sitting in my favourite chair, in my new permanent address, living with Terryl and writing these additional thoughts. Eight years have transpired since I became dreadfully ill with a host of issues that peeled 60 pounds off my once 205-pound body, demoralized my mind and put me in the hospital for a long time, but I recovered over the next twenty-four months largely due to Terryl, Greg, Rob, Dr Sayeed and several additional doctors who provided the necessary surgeries to put me on the path to recovery in March of 2017. Being of sound mind and body, I sold my too-large home with too many responsibilities in Brampton at the top of the market on April 30, 2017, and moved into a retirement facility consisting of retired folks, mostly in wheelchairs and walkers. Revera Greenway's nurses and staff took care of the rest for almost two years before I acted on the following suggestion from a lovely 94-year-old lady resident who, on learning my age, proclaimed "You're much too young to be living here." It took me several months for that thought to take hold and one day I spoke to Terryl and asked if she was still eager to do this, and she was. I made the arrangements with Greenway, and a mover named Courtney dispatched a truck and two guys to do the move on November 18, 2018. It was a breeze in no more than 5 hours and $550.00 cash money paid to Raheem and Randy with a two beer tip and they were gone and appreciated.]

Alexander McPope wants to jump in here and write about their Cruise on the Mediterranean. Thank you

The Med Aug 31 to Sept 24 2013

This trip came out of the blue, so to speak. While perusing the travel sites as he is wont to do there, it was: another Med Cruise too good to be true. So he jumped all over it and booked it after a short discussion with Terryl who said: "Are you kidding? Let's do it!"

What will follow will follow their return from Venice on September 26, 2013. Dear readers. There will be prose to die for; well, you know the rest.

They arrived home on September 26 right on time, and exactly one month to the date of departure to Barcelona, the site of the infamous robbery only two years ago, but this time they escaped unscathed and firmly intact. The start of the trip was a difficult time in that he had a cold and his right ankle wasn't working as it should. This would surely be a situation to slow them down and it did. You know that Terryl is capable of walking straight up the hill to Santorini in high heels: that has not changed. Gary, on the other hand, usually deals with at least

65

one ankle or knee requiring ultra sound and Skenar treatment on a semi-regular basis now.

He has provided me with a ton of photographs that I'm not allowed to place here, but here is a list of ports: Marseille, Livorno, Rome, Venice, Santorini, Athens, Kotor, Dubrovnik, and more over the 24 days.

These are Captions to his photos:

*On board drinking, having fun and watching the sun do its thing morning and evening.

*There is something about the wake of a great ship plowing through the water.

*The Grand Canal in Venezia; the most romantic ride you'll ever take in all the world in a black, gold and red Gondola.

*The gentleman with the paddle is a seventh-generation Gondolier with a wealth of local knowledge.

*Sailing away from Venezia on the 11th deck of Ms Nieuw Amsterdam, a magnificent ship three years in service.

*Buying a beautiful Pashmina in Istanbul and bargaining for Saffron in the Grand Bazar of Istanbul from Moustafa himself.

*The entrance Gate #1 to the Grand Bazar...don't get lost here. There are over 6000 shops in there and 18,000 sellers who never give up.

*Relaxing on board those great deck chairs on #3;

*The ruins of Ephesus; yes, those are toilet seats.

*The silk worms in Carpetium; their new Silk 1000 knots per square inch carpet.

*Santorini looking down from the top and up from the sea. The view as you see is the magic.

It would be inappropriate for me to continue dragging his Captions on and on and to place them here. If you are one who knows where he lives, why not go for a visit. Don't be shy. Just come on over and ask for me, *Alexander McPope,* who toils tirelessly and usually without compensation of any kind. He tells me that I'm lucky to be working. I guess that's true.

Oh, I almost forgot something he wrote while on board. Here it is pasted below. Perhaps you may get a kick out of these thoughts as well before they become an addition to *Alexander McPope's* work that he is so fond of.

Today is Sunday September 22, 2013 and the Med Cruise will end in two days' time. I am writing this while facing east from a deck lounging chair, the old type made of wood never painted but made comfortable by a spongy mat. The sun has been up for several hours, providing both sunshine and shade on the Promenade Deck 3 of the beautiful three-year-old Ms Nieuw Amsterdam. Several times during this voyage, I have thought about Thomas Mann and his book <u>Death in Venice</u> and especially when the protagonist is wrapped up in blankets during his sail into Venice. That time could never have been this time of year. We have enjoyed 25 to 34C degrees temperatures for the last 22 days and the honourable Mr Ansbach should have been with us enjoying himself rather than being on the verge of death. Dirk Bogart played this character in the movie of the same name; Mahler's music permeates the atmosphere throughout these tragic scenes: the complete opposite to my experience.

Several days ago, we met Branko and Nancy, who live in Amsterdam, he a Dutchman and she an American by birth met in the USA during Branko's post-university travels. Branco is a former World Champion Gymnast on the Pommel Horse. Nancy works for the Royal Bank of Scotland and they have two daughters aged 16 and 18. Our new friends are extremely fit and walk or run everywhere. We have enjoyed several meals together as well as the one tour in Ephesus. They have my card and I will have theirs before we part on Tuesday in Venice. Of course, the idea is to visit Amsterdam or Toronto sometime down the road. Terryl and Nancy compared recent purchases on the sail-a-way out of Santorini last night.

There is magic onboard a vessel cruising calm waters with food and drink at your beck and call 24 hours a day. Terryl said: "I feel quite wealthy right now." Her words are genuine, heartfelt and completely understood by me. She also says that she will never take what we have together for granted. So often we see couples who seem to do this. They also appear to be bored and uncomfortable with each other. Perhaps you have experienced a similar observation of a couple having a meal and never talking to each other. Sad, isn't it. We, however seem to be talking all the time. Here is guy named Bill who, at 86, sails the world as a single man. Debbie from Montana initially introduced him as Bill Clinton. [There is a nice little story accompanying the name change that can only be delivered orally.] Bill's wife passed away in 2006, right after Hurricane Katrina wiped out his boat in New Orleans. His son is a pilot with American Airlines providing Bill with the type of privileges that we enjoy with Air Canada. Bill too is a former sales executive. We meet on the back pool deck in the mornings. Bill is a great guy and Terryl wants to set him up with a lady. He'd like that too. Today is September 23, 2013 and I am typing this message on the deck. This morning the purple check out bag tags were delivered with a FAQ sheet that answers any questions one could ever have regarding disembarkation.

I was on the Lido pool deck at 6:05 to enjoy another perfect morning with plenty of sunshine, ready to climb over the mountains in the east in another few moments. Guess who walked out?… Bill did and we continued our conversation for an hour. Terryl joined us shortly thereafter. The conversation drifted by just as the water does only 9 decks below. Debbie's name came up as a possible lady friend for Bill somewhat down the road. Debbie had left the ship on September 12 and Bill had received an email from her yesterday. Terryl was excited about that and Bill delivered the following comment: "I'm not so sure that I want any repeat business." With that, we laughed heartily and knew exactly what he meant. Bill travels as a single on board HAL and has met his share of women who would have an interest in a charming fellow just like Bill Clayton.

Terryl begins to pack and the anxiety of getting her stuff in the suitcase builds…just like it always does, and of course, I ask her not to worry because I think I will have a little extra room in my bag. We will see how that works tonight. Giant crab legs are on the lunch menu along with all sorts of meats, chicken, fish, soups, vegetables and the like, exactly the same as yesterday and for the last 24 days. After another fill up, we head for the deck pool and see: Branko and Nancy from Amsterdam; Gary (a US Airway pilot) and Lisa from San Diego; Bill along with Margaret and Claudio from Adelaide, Australia, who we met at a cocktail party two nights ago. After another 30 minutes in the direct sun we look at the zillion photos they have taken of us at every opportunity. Some of them are fabulous but we delay the decision just one more time while they try to locate another batch of us. I'm on the starboard side of the ship, the shady side at the moment, and the screen is easy to see. Tonight there will be another meal on the Lido, perhaps the theatre to see the 6 candidates who are attempting to be the cruise winner of Dancing With The Stars: a contest that will award the grand prize of a complimentary cruise to the winner who will compete with others sometime in January 2014. The last cruise winner was a guy from Toronto who looked as professional as the professional who trained him. Terryl thinks he was a plant; maybe he was.

Just before Covid 19 turned our world and governments upside down, not to mention the economic and work place issues that changed our lives, Terryl and I were on a wonderful cruise from Dubai to Cape Town lasting a total of 50 days with seven days in Dubai and seven more in Cape Town. I started to keep a daily journal on that trip and sent it to family and friends. Many of those recipients thanked me for doing that and said many nice things like, "I felt like I was on the trip with you and Terryl."

This a whopper of a journal and I hope you enjoy it:

Toronto to Dubai to Mumbai to Cape Town to Toronto.

We met a low-key but effective cruise salesperson onboard Azamara Pursuit in January, 2019 who tried to whet our whistle for another ship board adventure. That's this one, or rather two going back to back from Dubai UAE to Mumbai India to Cape Town South Africa in 35 days. We'll spend several days in Dubai and then visit Doha Qatar, Sir Bani Yas, Muscat Oman, Abu Dhabi UAE and dock in Mumbai. We'll be overnight in Mumbai and then visit Cochin India, Victoria Seychelles, Praslin Seychelles, Mombasa Kenya, Zanzibar Tanzania, Maputo Mozambique, Richards Bay South Africa, Durban South Africa, Port Elizabeth South Africa and Cape Town South Africa. In total, if all goes well, we will be away from our beloved Port Credit for 50 days.

August 27, 2019 I visited three websites to purchase an e-visa for our four days in India. On the first one, the application was thorough in that they wanted one's parents' detail as well as the traveler. I thought that was a trifle overkill but I proceeded to complete the document and submit it. There's the rub; and I needed to call them if I needed help. After the usual 25-minute wait Mike picked up my call. I thought his manner was rough but he reluctantly walked me through his company's process. The form didn't reveal the cost so I asked what it was; he didn't know and put me on hold. Another long pause without the elevator music and he reappeared saying $360.00 for my application (he didn't even know about Terryl's) which would have followed. With that information, I thanked him and hung up. I looked at the other two companies and went with iVisa.com for $235.00 for the two of us. They tell me that I'll have my visa in two weeks. Additionally, the next confirmation came through and the money has been spent.

November 11, 2019 has us dealing with pneumonia for the fifth day. I have it and she cooks and makes me as comfortable as possible. The final plans such as a hotel in Dubai and Cape Town, plus a flight back to Dubai to meet our plane to Toronto from Dubai, have not been finalized. The only question is: will I be well enough to do the trip? Dr Wahba had me on triple-strength antibiotics and inhalers that we thought would do it. And they did. She cleared me to go. Full Stop.

It's December 1, 2019 and the final plans are in place. We will be staying at a small hotel in downtown Cape Town from January 21 to January 27 and then fly on Emirates from Cape Town to Dubai on January 27 and on to Toronto on January 28, 2020 with Air Canada.

After a wonderful Boeing 787 flight on AC56 we landed in Dubai and sailed through customs, baggage and duty-free with ten bottles of wine, and a taxi to Movenpick Jumeirah Beach Hotel. Every male or female service person treated us with extraordinary kindness, respect and dignity. This vacation has gotten off perfectly and after a good night's rest, we breakfasted in a nice little outdoor restaurant a few blocks from the hotel. Everyone has suggested that a Hop on Hop off bus as the start - something we usually do in most cities.

Today's ride features Dubai's Skyscrapers of which I hope my Apple 8's camera will do justice to this phenom all started just a few years ago and continues to flourish. You'll see a few cranes here and there.

UAE was nothing but rolling sand dunes.

"Fourty-seven years after its establishment in 1972, the UAE has become a shining country filled with soaring skyscrapers and architectural marvels. And the country owes its thanks to the remarkable ruling families of the UAE! The royal families of the UAE that serve as the country's rulers have built this brilliant place from the ground up, and are admired for their grace and dignity, hard work and charity. They also rank amongst the world's richest royal families - and some even have a massive fan base on Instagram." *(The preceding was written by MyBayut.)*

Of course these wonders would never have been without their oil. While riding along on the Hop-on Hop-off bus the narrator casually mentioned that 40,000,000,000 (billions) barrels of oil held in reserve will run out in the year 2040. Furthermore, the UAE is ranked among the top Financial Markets in the world along with London, New York and Hong Kong; and its Tourism business is booming internationally; here's a factoid, at one point, 40% of all the Cranes in the world were in Dubai and its immediate surrounds.

As we continue our journey, we find the service people are friendly and effective. Bartering is ingrained in their system. A little advice on this is to start at 50% of the asking price -- (which is very difficult to achieve because the objective is to warm you up to the point of buying, and then you still need to drag the asking price out of them) -- and then finally agree to buy it at slightly more, or less, than that.

I must add that the police are not in evidence here; there are people employed to help one in all manner of needs. We were leaving the huge Dubai Mall and wanted a taxi -- there was one idling by the curb and we approached him with a question, and with his answer, he said get in quickly. He could see an attendant of some kind approaching him and he said that his picture was taken by this fellow. The three of us were in the wrong place so he asked us to leave his cab. (Which we did.) The fines are serious: if you run a red light and an accident occurs the fine is 30,000 AED ($10,000.00 Canadian and loss of licence). I hope we didn't get him in trouble.

With two days left on our tour of Dubai UAE, the question raised is, what next? The answer is more of the same. In doing so, Terryl got quite a scare when purchasing some jewellery with her debit card. A salesperson presented the adjusted cost and accepted her card, but returned it with this comment: EMPTY. She tried it again with the same result and as might be the case, Terryl thought the worst: HACKED. And yes, once again these people were concerned and helpful without question. Together we called the Canadian Bank and after forty-five minutes, we were talking to a lady in Regina who advised that her money was still there. The next day it was the same result. However, when we visited a CitiBank establishment, she was able to get plenty of cash using the same card. A pleasant young man gave us his explanation and off we went. No problem...if it happens again, she will use my card. What?

By the way, the weather has been perfect all week at about 26 Celsius with mostly sun and a few wispy clouds. Apparently, the temperature can get to the mid 40's during the summer, but that doesn't stop the people from coming here. They had 15,000,000 come in 2018 and they spent $28,000,000,000.00 on the beach, in the sky, on the dunes, in the hotels, in the massive malls and on the golf courses too.

After a few hours at the Emirates Golf Club having breakfast, hitting range balls and chatting with staff members we taxied back to our hotel to get ready for lunch. What a life. What a pleasant day at the golf course, walking around the Jumeirah Beach district and closing with Happy Hour drinks, watching a cricket match and dinner on the Promenade.

Outside the Souq vendors are in their shops, ready to help you buy their wares. Inside the Souq these mostly young men are all over you with their precious jewels, herbs, textiles and an assortment of foods and other items. This kind of shopping at first is entertaining, however, one must know that this activity is the way their living is earned, and they have been doing this for a very long time. I believe they also enjoy bartering with their shoppers; they never want you to walk away without a sale; moreover, when the sale is not complete, there are no hard feelings that I could see. This is a fascinating place in Old Town Dubai.

And of course, back at Jumeirah Beach, we have the Bentleys and Lamborghinis all parked and in full view. So long Dubai, I think we'll be back.

After a seamless check-out of the Movenpick Jumeirah Beach Hotel, our baggage handler loaded our stuff into a Meter'd Taxi (he made a strong suggestion to avoid the black limo type) driven by a grandfather whose home was in Sudan, he asked if we would like some music and if it might be from his country? Our answer was of course; and off we went on a major 12-lane highway to the Port of Rashid. The ride took a little longer than I expected and cost $33.00 Canadian.

99.8% of all shipping arrives and leaves from the Port of Rashid which I swear goes on and on forever. One may think that with its size that there could be a problem finding our ship. We passed the Queen Elizabeth 11, the Jewel of the Seas and several others when we found the big A for Azamara docked and ready to board. We paid our friend from the Sudan and he helped the attendant load our stuff on to a cart destined for delivery to our balcony cabin 6075, after which we entered the terminal for registration. Terryl was amazed when the documents prepared for this trip came out of my case in the order requested by the staff who registered us and welcomed us on board. She said that this amazed her, and I said, 'It's a steep learning curve that has evolved over the twenty-odd cruises we have enjoyed."

On board, our first encounter is with Alina from Odessa, south of Ukraine, who is a totally engaging young woman with an entirely unique haircut and a small tattoo of an airliner on the inside of her left upper arm. And of course my beautiful Terryl strikes up a conversation after I asked if she was an Airline person prior to her work on the Azamara Cruise Ships. Her answer is no, along with a confession that she just loves to travel. Terryl's connection with Alina was instant. I'm guessing we'll be looking for this young lady to pour our drinks on many of the next 35 days of this voyage to Cape Town, South Africa.

I'm sitting on my balcony at 15:10 on December 17, 2019 which is approximately 3 hours after boarding the Azamara Quest. I'm inhaling another gin and tonic after two Budweisers and two Champagnes and sampling a plate of cheeses, Pad Thai, and a breaded chicken that thoroughly, if not completed, met my needs when a tug boat pulled up along side the Monjasa Performer Monrovia ship nestled along side the Quest. After several minutes I look again and there she goes. This is a beautiful cargo ship that has set sail from Dubai to ports unknown to me. My thought as she leaves her birth is that I know so little about this industry and shipping in general, and, that it's probably too late to learn any more. Dennis Casaccio, Daniel Loyd McDonald and Steve Ellis, son of Norm and Jeanette Ellis come to mind. These guys know plenty about this Industry: perhaps a word or two from one of these gentlemen to another in a position to get another started in an industry is all it took. Perhaps it helped to establish them in a position of authority. I like to think it so, just the way I was introduced to Duncan McGregor in 1963.

I'm sitting on my balcony at 17:00 on December 18 with a slight rumbling of our ship's motors and a gentle push and guidance by a perfect little tugboat and off we go to Doha, Qatar.

The Burj Khalifa driving through the clouds at 800+ metres is very visible.

Our body clocks are still discombobulated: it's 04:45 and we're wide awake. However, the Insider and Azamara never disappoint with access and service, such as the self-serve in the Windows Cafe with all types of speciality coffees, juices, fruit and cereals. It's done. I'm eating, drinking and in front of the MacBook Air typing away with Terryl propped up, watching her favourite of many world wide channels presented on board: this one is on specific wild life - lions, antelope, elephants, water buffalo, and others - all roaming in Africa and looking for water and food in their habitat.

I had not made any pre-arrangement for an excursion while in Doha, Qatar and I see one that looks interesting. They call it The North of Qatar with a duration of 7 hours showcasing their rich traditions, such as pearl diving, the ruins of Zubara Fort an ancient fortress for a fascinating look at archaeology in action. The other offerings are a wild ride through the dunes described as a roller coaster sensation, and strenuous too. We don't need any more back pain. It also describes hanging out in tents and carpets covering the desert, perhaps a little like the Bedouin. They offer a trip to Souq Waqif and a museum for 4 hours.

Ship Excursions opens on schedule and we are on; we'll meet our fellow travellers on Deck 5 in the Cabaret Lounge at 08:45, and off we go. Here's an odd fact: on the way from Dubai to Doha, the clocks go back one hour, and from Doha to Sir Bani Yas the clock goes forward that one hour. And these are very short distances between places. Odd, I thought.

Today we are anchored off Sir Bani Yas, which is primarily a wild life sanctuary with half of its area set aside for conservation. Azamara is using their Tenders to float the passengers back and forth. Terryl and I have decided to take a pass on this man-made island sanctuary and hit the gymnasium for a first workout in Azamara's beautifully outfitted and handsomely designed facilities. This was one of my commitments because I just wasn't doing it at home. My 'Sport's Medicine Doctor' had recommended Physiotherapy and/or Acupuncture to relieve some of my issues and concerns, for which I did receive 5 sessions of Acupuncture as well as a few exercises from a chiropractor named Neil. His treatment is all well and good, but I really don't think there's anything like old fashion gym work, especially for me.

I'm now in Azamara Quest's beautiful Library, which is on the top deck occupying the width of the ship and a depth of thirty-five feet and completed by comfortably padded chairs, deep coloured wooden tables, soundproofing carpets below painted-coffered ceilings and of course, numerous walls of books and materials housed in mahogany shelving. A perfect place for doing exactly what I'm doing.

It's about 12:20 and Terryl and I will meet at 13:00 for a small little drink, perhaps a tidbit or two and discuss the tour, of which there are several options, that we will take while in Abu Dhabi tomorrow. Its feature is and probably always will be their Grand Mosque boasting over 80 domes, four 350-foot-high minarets, and 100,000 tons of white marble rising above manicured gardens. This sacred place will accommodate 40,000 faithful. The rules upon entering are strict with regard to appropriate dress and the use of cameras. One small consideration newly minted is that one's shoes may now be left on when entering the Grand Mosque.

Last evening was delightful. Both of us deliberated over the Shore Excursions options and marked the ones we wanted. In Abu Dhabi, it's today at 13:30 for the 'Grand Mosque Visit', and on December 23 it's 'Panoramic Muscat' in Muscat, Oman at 08:15; and then in Mumbai, India on December 27 at 09:00, it's 'Mumbai on the Move' when many of the passengers will disembark and head for the airport.

We met a nice couple before dinner who originated in Scotland for Roger and China for Ilia. They now live and work in Bahrain and had plenty of information about their working and social lives as ex-pats. We will be sitting down with them at dinner sometime soon. Our meal in the Discoveries room was delicious, the entertainment in the Cabaret featuring songs by Stephen Millet was very nice - Stephen also subs as Assistant Cruise Director - and we ended up in the Living Room listening and dancing to the Fancy Triplets: three young women singing and playing saxophone, guitar and keyboard.

And today, all passengers were asked to pick up their passports, leave the ship and surrender them to UAE customs. At that point, one could go about their activities in Abu Dhabi. Our trip in Abu Dhabi will start this afternoon at 13:30, so we passed through the terminal building and went back on board for breakfast.

Our tour of the Grand Mosque was exceptional in that it is perhaps the most important thing that one must see when visiting the sister city to Dubai, and that is the capital city Abu Dhabi in the UAE. Our driver took us through tunnels and over bridges that appeared to be quite new, and as is the case, spotless. He detailed the area's relevancy to the Ruler's master plan as well as its Islamic religious dominance of their population which is 20% by birthright, with the expats running at 80%. He talked about the young adult when getting married is given a significant amount to have the wedding of their dreams, a full amount of money to buy their first home, and a few additional contributions to get their young marriage off on the right foot. We are amazed at what appears to be factoids about their country. They don't pay taxes, but if they can afford to give 2.5% of their earned or inherited net worth, it is a one-time only donation to charity, and their medical plan is also their birthright and paid by the rulers.

And again the cranes on buildings being constructed are many in the city centre and blossoming in the outskirts. The bridges and tunnels are already built to handle the growing population - the expats are doing the grunt work and the well-educated Emirates are calling the shots. In every business activity controlled by foreign investment, there are mandated locals working in the administration office of these firms: it's the law.

The weather at this time of year is in the mid 20's Celsius and higher than the mid 40's in the summer. For us, I'm sure their summer conditions would be unbearable, but for now, the air is warm, the sky is blue, the Azamara Quest is the place to be.

Last night we partied at the White Night event with a fabulous buffet on the pool deck topped off with Crepes smothered in sweets and cognac, and had an early night to sleep-in while we sail toward Muscat, Oman for our docking on December 23, 2019.

We arrived within minutes of our schedule and hustled up to the Windows Cafe for a nice breakfast of Pancakes and Fruit for me, with eggs and fruit for Terryl. Jamie dropped by and apologized for missing our cocktail and dinner engagement the other night; he was bushed and took a nap and slept right through the appointed hour. Totally understandable, and we had another nice chat with this 81-year-old practising Psychiatrist from New York City before heading to the gangway and our Oman Tour Guide, who had us for the next 4 hours.

The capital city of Muscat, and the country of Oman is a well-run Muslin empire whose current ruler is Sultan Oaboos the son of the previous ruler who relinquished his crown in 1970. Sultan Oaboos has ruled for 49 years and if he can overcome his recent illness will celebrate 50 years as the supreme religious and governmental leader of Oman in 2020. Once again oil and gas are 90% of their GDP, with tourism and editable dates completing their working lives. Earlier we talked about the citizens loving their leader. Sultan Qaboos is no exception; for example, when he was younger and healthier, he would ride through the villages tossing money out on to the streets for any and all to use as they wished. No strings attached, just like their current practice of giving plenty of money to their citizens for marriage costs, home purchases et al. Remember, they have no income tax payable by the citizens and their medical and educational costs are born by the government, and the government is Sultan Qaboos. Our tour guide tells us that everyone loves this man who has no children to pass on the Royal Baton. So when the time is right, he will appoint a member of his collective family, such as a cousin or a nephew. [Two months after our cruise docked in Cape Town, we heard the news that Sultan Qaboos passed away; his funeral was attended by many world leaders because he was a respected, confident and accomplished man loved by his people.]

We are back on the ship after seeing the outside of their Grand Mosque, a certain Palace that Sultan Qaboos uses for guests, an incredible Opera house, a Souk (unfortunately with water running down one of its pathways from a broken water main), but just in time to get some jewellery to die for and two additional Pashminas for incredibly low bartered prices. The sellers enjoy this system just like the rest of us foreign shoppers.

Last night was an amazing evening compliments of Azamara Cruise Line that bussed us to Muscat's huge new Convention Centre by the Airport. Once again Captain Filip greeted us as we entered a magnificent auditorium to hear a five-piece authentically Muslim band, followed by fourteen piece brass band, both playing their favourite works to the delight of all who attended. In a little over an hour we drove to the ship, where the party had already started with more food and music and drinks to be had in several venues.

Today Terryl and I shuttle-bussed it back to the Souk to purchase a few little goodies and immediately were at a loss to find the store of choice: a gold shop with our ears, necks and wrists begging to be adorned. Alas, I gave up and walked out of the Souk with the guidance of many vendors, and when seated with a drink Terryl went back in and then, came out fourty minutes later claiming no success once again.

Now we're on the ship - have had a nice little lunch with refreshments - and preparing for the sail away at 17:00 and of course, the party to follow. In about sixty-four hours we'll dock in Mumbai, India.

Last night, Christmas Eve, Terryl and I agreed to meet Jamie for a drink followed by dinner at the Discoveries Bar and Dining room. This time he was there and we easily launched into another spontaneous and lively discussion about life, illnesses, family and cruising. Jamie is the same man we had drinks with very early in this 11-day cruise to Mumbai. When we stood to announce our readiness to dine Jamie says, "We're five for dinner please." Terryl and I looked at each other with surprise that we were now five. These two additional gentlemen were not; Jamie had prearranged that too. So off we go and when seated Roberto and Alfredo introduced themselves as did we. They are originally from Cuba and have been living together in Miami for twenty years. And of course they were pleasant and well spoken with their Cuban accent still in evidence. The food was wonderful and the service was even better. Just before the main course was brought to our table Jamie excused himself and said he was a little tired and was going to his cabin. The four of us finished the dinner together and departed as friends.

The show last night was a little like an old-fashioned Bing Crosby family gathering with all kinds of performers on stage singing, playing guitars and telling Christmas stories until well into the night. We were tired by 23:00 and went to our cabin just before midnight.

This morning a beautiful Christmas Brunch was laid out in the Discoveries Dining Room where we enjoyed Crab Legs, Lox, Lamb Chops, Fruits and so much more all presented beautifully under an Ice Sculpture slightly higher than head high. Another start to an Azamara day at sea where the temperature has been a steady 25 degrees Celsius and sunny since we landed in Dubai fifteen days ago. Many of our fellow passengers will be disembarking and heading for the Mumbai Airport on December 28, but not us, we have 38 additional days before we fly to Dubai from Cape Town, South Africa, on Emirates Air and then to Toronto on Air Canada.

Last night was one where both of us were tired - we really wanted to be alone together - and had a very light dinner on the outdoor Patio, which is always a delight. I had an appetizer of Carpaccio artistically prepared, especially for me, and Terryl had a tiny piece of chicken, providing the energy required to take the elevator to our cabin. There is a music-only channel on our television that did the trick, and we were asleep in no time.

This morning we got up at 08:30 just in time to get dressed and out on the Pool Deck to see (with special glasses provided by Azamara) the complete Solar Eclipse, an episode that lasted two hours with the maximum effect visible at 09:15. The Deck was full of passengers with a staff member describing the visual effect in technical detail.

Professor Chuck Richardson lectured at 10:00 on 'Mumbai: Gateway To India' complete with his photographs yielding a valuable precursor to our visit scheduled for December 27, 2019. His delivery was as expected dotted with explanations of population, poverty, working children, and of the very wealthy going about their business in the fastest-growing GDP in the world, even ahead of China. The Professor discussed India's political scene before and after India's independence from Britain. But most importantly, his focus was on their working children who should have been in school, along with the working adult poor's need for employment which keeps them using ancient tools instead of modern equipment. Why? If new equipment requires one person to do the same task as ten then what would the replaced nine do to earn a living? This is a direct opposite thought process that is used in North American and many other areas in the world. He also instructs that 80% Hindu population is quite happy doing what they do because the real rewards in life come to them in the afterlife. Full Stop.

From 14:00 for an hour in the Cabaret, the entire singing and dancing team entertained us with fabulous and familiar songs from Broadway Shows. They were terrific and this their penultimate show was performed to a packed house who truly appreciated an extraordinary performance.

This is the day we dock in Mumbai, India at 07:00 and make ready to enter this amazing stand-alone Metropolis of 22,000,000 people. Terryl's recollections going back to the 1980's are well known - and they are not pretty. Memories of children with limbs broken and bent begging in the streets, others stealing from your pockets, crushing crowds continuously moving, men lying in the streets, and even dead babies lying in the gutters, and a certain unpleasant smell emanating from everywhere was constant. Terryl recalls gifting pens and little trinkets to give to the little ones, and to one crippled child she and her fellow Air Canada friends gave a set of crutches one week only to find they had been sold to buy food the following week. All sad but true.

Our tour this morning entitled 'Mumbai on the Move' declared that things have changed somewhat in fourty years. I recognize that a four-hour bus tour only skirts the heart of a major city like Mumbai, but it was enough for Terryl to state with certainty that Mumbai really is on the move. All of India's GDP is the fastest growing in the world, even faster than China. The streets are much cleaner, we saw only one man lying down in the street, only one or two children begging, and lines of children walking in formation in school uniforms. We saw much of what has not changed too: prepared lunches arriving by 11:00 via bicycle messenger by the thousands, dozens of men pounding other people's laundry in cement tubs and then hanging it out to dry in the sun. Both occupations have survived modern process and procedure for decades. One theory is that why to replace employment with machinery that only costs more money for electricity, and most importantly, puts men out of work. We were told that more young Indians are receiving better education now more than ever, and that the divorce rate for 'love marriage' is going up and up while 'arranged marriage' is staying as low as ever.

We toured Mahatma Gandhi's home (now a museum) to view photographs, letters and events that form and speaks to his incredible life in service to his fellow citizens. Of course, there are volumes written on Gandhi: one letter above all that caught my eye was Gandhi's letter to Adolph Hitler beginning:

"Dear Friend…Friends have been urging me to write to you for the sake of humanity. But I have resisted their request, because of the feeling that any letter from me would be an impertinence…" *[How wonderful and humble can one man can be?]*

This evening Jamie dropped by the Spirits Bar and jumped into a last drink with us. Of course he had a few stories, one fairly risqué, mostly about his time in Leavenworth Prison (as a Doctor, not an inmate), which prompted me to launch my 1960 Cincinnati Workhouse Prison escape with John McCusker along with its trial and eventual outcome. On leaving us for the last time, Jamie handed Terryl a piece of folded paper and stated, "Oh, here's a message for you." I opened it and read his name, telephone and email address in Washington D.C. What a class act: Jamie's way of saying I want to see you again.

That evening we exchanged emails with the Ainslie couple from Vancouver, and the Boyer couple from Dallas, friendly people indeed, and one of the ladies was a former Air Canada flight attendant. How good is that.

This morning approximately 440 passengers disembarked - we were two of sixty continuing on to Cape Town - and approximately 600 coming aboard for this twenty-four-day cruise to Cochin, India, two stops in Seychelles, (Kenya has been cancelled due to internal unrest

84

and conflict), stops in Tanzania, Mozambique, and four stops in South Africa with final disembarkation in Cape Town. The crew, including navigational, service and administration, is not changing. (It's nice that we know many of them by face and name now.)

We have returned our room key, and received our new room keys, in a seamless process identifying us as back-to-back passengers to begin enjoying the day on board. Terryl and I discussed taking another tour of Mumbai today and decided against it after speaking with fellow passengers who had visited what they call the 'slum' area yesterday. After hearing their comments, Terryl said, "After 40 years this part of Mumbai has never changed."

We sailed away from Mumbai last night at 17:00, this visit provided a whole new look into a fascinating culture, one that survives in millions of lives, and another where their lot is improving through education and adoption of Western ideas and concepts put into practice.

Terryl made an inquiry at the Spa for which she was invited to participate in a lucky draw. The Gym area, next to the Spa, was crowded and after a few comments extolling the virtues and relaxing feelings their work provides, the first lucky number was pulled and 6075 (our cabin) received a $75.00 treatment. My arms went up and a loud noise of some kind covered the room. Terryl's name was on the card and she was thrilled and gave a warm and respectful thank you to all those present.

This morning we are cruising south toward the tip of India and will dock at Cochin, India, tomorrow morning. The sea is calm, the pollution is gone, the food continues to be excellent along with super service by attendants who know our preferences and react accordingly. Read, relax, enjoy is the name of the game for these 38 hours sailing to Cochin.

Last night we had a drink with Teresa and Tracy in the Living Room on Deck 10 facing south as we cruised to Cochin. Terryl had met them the other night and invited them for a drink. For one hour, the conversation was constant and lively, detailing many adventures on the high seas, including a robbery at gunpoint in Mexico City. This is not a pretty story; They and their luggage were followed from the airport and pulled over by a look-a-like police vehicle, and with a gun forced into the side of Teresa's head, were frisked, and verbally accosted while their personal possessions as well as the contents of several luggage bags were taken and loaded into their vehicle. Their passports were not taken. Why? Because these criminals wanted their targets to get back on a plane asap and not report the crime to the authorities. They are well-healed, retired for 11 years and have a home in Dallas as well as Mexico, and as of last night have spent the last 99 days on board the Azamara Quest as she travels the world.

This morning, while docked in Cochin we have cleared Indian Customs (again) and will begin a tour entitled 'Walk the Broadway Market followed by a sundowner at Taj Malabar Hotel' this afternoon at 16:45; this will take us well into the night and then back to the ship. Currently, we are having a cool drink onboard.

Let's begin with last night: at 16:45 outside the terminal the bus attendants came to find us, because we had not picked up our #10 chest sticker prior to leaving the ship. (I need to tell you that our instructions did not include that little detail - incidentally, the first time this has happened on this trip with Azamara.) So off we go into the city of Cochin or Kochi which, ever you prefer, that is teeming with motor bikes, and Tuk-Tuks (three-wheel motorbikes with room for two passengers in the back), buses, few private cars and loads of people with some on the move and others hardly moving. Our Tour guide talks and then the microphone quits, he taps it and he's off again. His is giving us some of the history of Cochin and the 28 states in all of India. India's President Modi runs the show but he needs help to do his job for 1,400,000,000 of his fellow citizens, (only China is greater) and he does this with 28 Prime Ministers where some states are richer than others. Hundreds of years ago spices were the number one product India exported around the world with Pepper being the largest and most profitable for India. Today, it's still the most popular among the dozens and dozens of spices India grows and ships everywhere.

Our tour included a few stops, and what I concluded to be about a one-mile walk through the narrowest of streets filled with vendors politely selling their goods. For me it was difficult to keep up with him holding his sign over his head, as I continued to drip with sweat while side-stepping the pot holes and loose slabs of worn concrete. Terryl asked, "Are we going to stop and shop sometime soon?" Of course, we'll do whatever you ask was his reply. In due course no one, especially me, really wanted to shop in this local. The end of our tour was a stop at The Taj Malabar Hotel, a quite luxurious hotel on the water with a comfortable outside sitting area with nicely dressed waiters serving a really cold local beer that made my day. After a pleasant rest stop we were back on the ship for a late dinner in Windows Patio.

This morning after a little breakfast, we left the ship, and before we passed immigration, a nice young man reached over a small barricade and called, "Gary and Terry I'm here waiting for you." We went out to greet him and hopped into his Tuk-Tuk and headed for the Old Town past Jew Country (no kidding, it's still called that even though all have left for Israel and other parts of the world over the last century or more). We were driven to three shops, very nice shops, where the prices were higher, the selections were greater, and the service was friendly with kind words like, "I'm not trying to sell you anything, I'm just doing my job." After the third shopping stop, the driver asked if we'd like to shop for spices, or, if we'd like to go anywhere else in Cochin (all for the same price of $15.00 US). We had been with him for two hours by this time, so we thanked him and asked to go to the ship.

At 13:45 I'm sipping on a cold beer and writing this copy. Tonight is New Year's Eve and we don't have to ask about this evening's entertainment because the Azamara Quest has it all laid out in the dining room first, followed by the countdown extravaganza around the pool deck and its' bars, and a fabulous sail-a-way after midnight toward Seychelles with fireworks galore.

It's 12:45 (my body clock says 14:15) and I've recovered quite nicely from Azamara's New Year's Eve extravaganza beginning with a fabulous meal shared with Gloria (New York City) and Brian (London, UK). Terryl had been speaking with them earlier where we had my third martini at the Discovery Bar. The four of us were dining late by appointment and Terryl suggested we ask for a table for four. They agreed enthusiastically. Gloria declined the first table offered and accepted the next and we settled in, overlooking the passing ocean below. Again, the food was sublime and our conversation was agreeable. Gloria and Terryl were non stop and periodically joined Bryan and myself to quickly return to their topic of choice. Tonight was the second time Trump (Donald J) entered any conversation on the entire trip. Brian knew his current events and much of the USA as well. He likes Boris Johnson and would have voted for Trump if he'd been a US citizen. Brian articulated interesting points of view on these and other democratic leaders from several additional countries. We were the last group to leave the dining room at 23:30 to go to the Pool Deck where the music, dancing, fireworks and sail-away from Cochin had begun. It was a party that many passengers and crew enjoyed without question. It was 'hopping' up there! And again Terryl and I were the last to leave at 02:00 January 1, 2020. For me an incredible end to another very fine year I've been blessed to have lived.

The New Year Brunch began at 09:30 with the centre of the dining room filled with foods from around the world: crab legs and claws, fruits of many kinds sliced before your eyes, cheeses, eggs prepared any way you wish, lamb chops, pickled herring and much more, all served with as many Mimosa's and Specialty Coffees one could possibly ask for.

I'm writing this in the Drawing Room where it's quiet, and soon the Gym will beckon because I need it badly. I had promised myself to faithfully work out everyday, and as of now, I'm running at five days out of the fourteen we've been on board the Azamara Quest which is four days more than Terryl; but then she really is in much better shape and condition than me. Ten minutes on the bike at level 6, three sets of squats against a flat wall, three sets of arm-chest pushes and shoulder lifts with hand weights slightly heavier than last time and I was out and in The Living Room enjoying an iced Sparkling Water (no beer today until much later) after a fast 40 minutes in the Gym completing workout number six.

Azamara has a cruise/golf package about once a month on at least one of their three ships whereby they coordinate their cruise with a Golf Specialty company for a package deal consisting of five or six golf games with all the arrangements made at each of the different golf courses included in the itinerary. There is one on this ship starting the day we dock in Cape Town. The price at this time is discounted significantly for the 11-day cruise from Cape Town and back at five fabulous South African courses. Gary Player and Ernie Els are behind at least two of them. I thought about it, and then said no because we had sightseeing planned for the seven days we are in Cape Town. Maybe another time.

The highlight last night was in the theatre where Tom Seals played Boogie, the Blues and fourty-five minutes of fantastic piano and songs entertaining a packed house. Tom dresses plainly to say a lot about his presence, however he has a kind of Elton John appearance without the feathers, hats and wild eyeglasses. And when asked about it post show he said, "Many have said that I should introduce something along those lines." I bought his CD and will have it in the car when we are home. He's a great entertainer that should be heard by any that like his brand of music. At the end of his performance he ripped into The Flight of the Bumblebee with his right hand and Boogied with his left - a fascinating sound that requires plenty of talent and practice I'm sure.

Yesterday was also a slow day for us, and a great deal slower for many passengers who partied hardy the night before last.

We continue 210 degrees southwest for the second day (it's four days from Cochin, India to Seychelles) under pleasant warm conditions. For breakfast this morning Terryl suggested we might take a table in the sun, when Sundeep one of our favourites said don't do it and added that we might be okay for a few minutes but in the sun it was to hot to enjoy our meal. Sundeep is quite young and comes from India, Terryl hugs him and I give him the closed fist hand shake recommended by Azamara to avoid passing on little buggies (of the bacterial type between passengers). He will be tipped (and so will Ihor) even though tipping is included in all of Azamara's cruises as a matter of policy: one of the many attributes that attracts us to this cruise line.

Yesterday at 14:00 Chuck Richardson's lecture <u>The Intriguing Indian Ocean</u> was all about those Tectonic Plates on the move over the life of this planet's billions of years. This movement changes everything - albeit slowly - and it continues under our current Climate Change issues today. Among other things the warm waters of the Indian Ocean are moving into the Atlantic Ocean and the fish will go with it. I suppose this occurrence is not commonly spoken of, nor are the shifting plates causing Earthquakes and Tsunamis a hot topic. We are caught up on our Carbon Footprint and Plastic containers that will take 200 years to disintegrate, and the melting ice that will begin to eat away at our shorelines causing millions of citizens of many countries to move inland where the oceans have not gone….yet. In my view, scientists and even Mark Carney the former Auditor General of Canada, and now the newest money guru of the United Kingdom are right: we had better do what we are capable of doing to protect our citizens and the planet, and to do it now. But will the politicians yield to their growing scientific knowledge and guide the world's people at this time as the Tectonic Plates move a couple of inches and Earth's inevitable change?

Today we continue to sail toward Seychelles under wispy clouds, blue sky and blazing sun at a temperature of 86 degrees Fahrenheit. Terryl will spend her Spa winnings on a nail fill at 14:00 and I will read and stay in the shade.

Terryl has made friends with Captain Filip's wife and six-year-old daughter and we will soon have dinner with Nicola and Marianna while Filip drives the ship, makes the announcements, and generally is everywhere doing the job that he is very good at. Captain Filip also picked two of my photos for first prize in the Funny and Christmas categories. In acceptance, I did not mention the grand prize-winning category on our Antarctic cruise in January 2019. I owe much to the Apple iPhone and the crew at Apple Store in Sherway who hooked me on photography and the digital process.

On cruise vacations, one meets people; some you take to right away, and some you don't. Last night we bumped into Sandy and Cathy Aitken - right away - in the Discoveries Bar where we enjoyed a couple of drinks and lively conversation until one of us suggested we get a table for four. Sandy and Cathy are Scottish from Chapelhall, Airdrie which is east of Glasgow. They are over 60 years, own and run a B&B highly rated by Trip Advisor, and Cathy has a medical condition similar to Terryl's that has them discussing remedies and a host of other issues. Sandy and I enjoyed talking politics and sports including plenty of golf until The Royalty subject came up, and then the four of us jumped in. It was fun and informative and the evening flew by.

Elton John's music by the Quest singers and dancers rounded out the early evening. Unexpectedly, Terryl said let's hear a little music in

The Living Room and before we even sat down I started to dance and Terryl quickly followed and the room came alive. She still dances as well as ever - and loves it too.

A select group of Azamara guests were invited to a specially restaurant Prime C for brunch hosted by Captain Filip and several of his Officers and Crew. We were greeted by our hosts and taken to our table and a Mimosa for two was there in an instant with coffee a few moments later. The food was distinctly sumptuous with variety, beautifully displayed and served by excellent waiters. A great start to our day.

We are crossing the Equator at 16:00 today with a ceremony planned on the Pool Deck. This is day four of our At Sea experience and will dock tomorrow at 08:00 at Seychelles. People say this is a magnificent place on Earth, one that you will love and never forget.

We arrived on schedule in Seychelles on a gorgeous morning under a blue sky filled with the most unusual cloud formation: all white with abundant coverage and an almost wall-like abrupt finish off the coast of our arrival in the Port of Victoria. Terryl has arranged a meeting with Gloria and Brian to hire a taxi and drive around to the tourist highlights and then luncheon at some swanky spot to be determined.

Seychelles is a country made up of 115 islands with a population of 95,000 citizens with 85% of them living on one island Mahe; and the capital (Victoria) is here as well. The temperature ranges between 24 and 32 degrees Celsius all year long, and the drinking water is safe.

Down the gangplank, we go to face only three gentlemen offering tours in their air-conditioned vehicles. I spoke with the first and his English was excellent and spoken enthusiastically about his Mahe Island. Somehow our focus was redirected to another man whose price was $25.00 less, and he was selected for our tour. On the trip he spoke infrequently and incoherently about the sights we were seeing, and at the same time he wanted to please and did his best while the air was turned on and off too many times as requested by the ladies - mostly the other lady in the back two seats while her escort was seated in the front. We saw one of their beaches which was as clean as a whistle with turquoise-coloured water going out for 100 yards before it turned blue. And there are too many beaches to mention here. Mahe appears to be about 60 minutes from east to west, of wild turning roads going up and down hills that pass small houses and snack shacks on one side and another one that has ritzy hotels commanding the best views of their magnificent waters and mountainous terrain filling the island's centres. A look at two Tortoise displays with signage proclaiming 200 year old animals was delightful. These are pet-able creatures who are fed and kept captive just for people like us.

Mahe greets its visitors with four giant windmills indicating they're doing their part dealing with Climate Change. The island is clean and appears to be well managed by those who call the shots 4 degrees south of the Equator.

Creole is their first language but of course English is taught in their schools as well. They claim that Seychelles is one of the riches of African Countries - and that they are the happiest of people living on the African Continent. Our driver mentioned that this and that and the other are all paid for by the government, and furthermore when he retires he receives a 450 Euro pension for life.

Azamara Quest left Mahe Island with a bang last night; they did it with a huge party that began with a fabulous Buffet dinner on the Pool Deck complete with local musicians and dancers that performed well into the night. Everyone seemed to be dancing except Terryl and me: we were bushed from the tour we had throughout Mahe and hit the sack by 22:00.

Today, once again the sun rose in a majestic sky with billowing clouds overlaying the island of Praslin, and we were on the tender by 10:00

sharp. After a fifteen-minute 100-passenger tender ride and an Azamara arranged air-conditioned bus (the temperature had to be 88 degrees F) for another 15 minutes, we were on the pristine beach that put our Maché Beach into second place. We have seen, sensational water colours from beach sand, turquoise water, slowly developing light to darker blues that melt against the tropical skies of this Paradise. Suffice it to say that Praslin Island deserves the excellent beach resort reputation it has, and by us, one that it truly deserves. This beach had it all including shade, and no one pushing drinks down your throats either.

We will begin sailing towards the second stop on the African Continent at 15:00 today. The weather promises to co-operate with no Cyclones or Tectonic Shifts in the forecast.

'Big Red' Meghan Murphy was on our tender yesterday afternoon - and on stage last night in a heavily sequin red dress belting out show tunes made famous by Ethel Merman and Barbara Streisand. When we spoke with her on the tender I asked, 'are you the advertised entertainer tonight?' She is a Chicago native traveling the Cruise circuit and loving it; however, getting to Seychelles by air had her missing connections here and there, and this time one of them lost her luggage. Her show stuff is never checked in, just like our medicine, and she was able to perform last night and did it beautifully.

This morning we are on course 240 southwest ploughing through smooth seas for the entire day with a few appointments, one being at 14:00 for Chuck Richardson's Lecture Destination, Dar es Salaam which is our first stop in Tanzania, and another in the Cabaret Lounge at 20:15 with Stephen Millett and his song stylings. The rest of the day will be spent r.w.e.d. Reading Writing Eating Drinking and a little gym work for me.

Dar es Salaam is a translation of Cosmopolitan House of Peace, where 4.4 million people live. For interest's sake, Lagos has 21 million and

Cairo has 20.1 million as the largest cities in Africa. The Germans invested in this land through a company called the German East African Company only to lose it to the British after WW1. The British used Indian labour at low low labour costs and over time the Indians have become affluent in this city of Dar es Salaam. The politics at one time leaned toward socialism but since the 1980's Capitalism has directed their lives. 61% are Christians and 41% are Muslims. The language is Swahili spoken by 350 million with dozens of dialects trailing behind. John Magufuli is their President and is up for reelection in 2020 with a platform on anti-corruption and anti-family planning.

China has been their largest trading partner for the last three years because they want their rare minerals to make computers. Pretty smart those Chinese, eh?

All the above is courtesy of Thomas Jefferson who said, "He who receives an idea from me, receives instruction himself without lessening mine; as he who lights his taper at mine, receives light without darkening mine." And of course, Mr Chuck Richardson who is paid by Azamara to travel the world talking about what he has learned just for people like you and me.

We met Ron and Bonnie from Vancouver Island last night, actually we had met on December 28, 2019 at the Spa's draw for free services during this voyage. Bonnie's name had been drawn one minute after she left for the rest room. 'You must be here to win' was their reply, so I said she was just here a minute ago and I think she should have it, don't you? They gave it to Ron and he remembered me which led to a lively conversation about our lives and country.

A fascinating rainbow circled the sun yesterday afternoon for an hour or more, and Captain Filip, during his daily ship's status report, spoke of the process of water forming into crystals circling the sun to create such a magnificent image a few degrees south of the Equator.

Today, we continue sailing to Dar es Salaam under cloudy skies and continuing warm air over smooth seas.

At 14:00 Chuck Richardson lectured on Zanzibar a semi autonomous part of Tanzania with Stone Town forming the other part. And yes the tectonic plates were at work 14 million years ago to split it off the mainland and form the islands. Stone Town attracts the tourists, possibly because it was a big part of the Slave Trade operation where these poor native souls where made to march carrying Ivory Tusks and other items from their homelands where all would be sold including themselves in the city of Stone Town. Oddly enough the greatest slave trader was an Indigenous native named Tippu Tip (1832 to 1905) who owned the most slaves. Today an Anglican Church is also built on the sight of The Slave Memorial in Stone Town.

Freddie Mercury of Queen fame was born in Zanzibar in 1946 and the city has appropriate places acknowledging his life where Swahili is spoken, child mortality rate is 21% and life expectancy is 57 years. Take note of the spikes on some of the ancient large doors; they're there to stop the Elephants from crashing into and knocking the doors down.

We are in the city of Dar es Salaam, home of 4.4 million people, docked, breakfasted, down the gangplank, and on a complimentary bus to the swanky Hyatt Regency Hotel by 10:00. This is our meeting place for Azamara's passengers who are on their own (without an Azamara sponsored tour) in Dar es Salaam. After a little discussion with an attendant who fronted a taxi system we were on our way to Tinga Tinga Indigenous Art Centre. The ride was about thirty minutes revealing the city centre, the shore line with its huge sand bar, apartment buildings with laundry drying in the 85 degree Equatorial sun. We had an air-conditioned cab for ten dollars per person including an hour's wait and the drive back to the Hyatt.

Every Artisan we met and spoke with was courteous and politely invited us to view and take photos. Their art was poignantly African: large and small, framed or rolled, sculpted or painted, but most of all, impressive and artistic. Unfortunately we couldn't purchase a piece or two due to our lack of their currency, or the exact amount in USA dollars for which there was no change available from these charming, industrious and friendly people. For us we met only delightful and courteous artists who live for their work. But of course Trade and Barter are in play and important to their wellbeing. Perhaps our next stop in Tanzania will have us prepared to purchase and bring something home.

Early in the morning several little boats manned by Zanzibar's young people buzz by our ship waving in a welcoming way: this was a nice start to our two days in Zanzibar and Stone Town. We enjoyed a quick breakfast and off the ship we go to ride the complimentary bus into Stone Town where the usual characters are waiting to offer tours to the high points of interest for $20 dollars. Again we decide to hoof it just a hundred yards to, guess what, more locally made paintings, sculptures and the like that tourists need to see, and then bring home the stuff. We passed the Tembo Hotel and decided to enter the lobby and pass through to the beach where guests were swimming, sunning and generally enjoying the scenery and the hotel's amenities. Along the shoreline about twenty yards we found lounge chairs, tables and chairs, and benches under massive trees with huge leaves which, in a matter of minutes, protected us from the rain that suddenly appeared out of nowhere. Terryl was invited to join a young man who was waiting for his parents and a planned tour. He was a lawyer who studied at the University of Toronto and lives in Vancouver. A delightful person who was eager to know more about us and why we were in Zanzibar. His mother had lived here; she and her family were revisiting for the first time in over 40 years.

The temperature was in the high 80's, and with sweat dripping off my nose Terryl suggested we return to the ship and take another run at

Stone Town tomorrow. But for today, we passed and photographed Freddie Mercury's home and visited numerous craft shops, dropped into a small bank to break a few larger dollar amounts into smaller ones, and really enjoyed talking and joking with Stone Town's citizens. We'll take a little taxi for the big tour planned for tomorrow.

After last night's Ribeye Steak grilled perfectly in the Patio dining area, two Vodkas with a splash of triple sec and lime juice in the Den we hit the sack.

And this may hold some interest for you: I used the ship's ATM yesterday to acquire USA Dollars for various reasons. The bills popped out as usual. Late last night, I was informed that my USA Visa card had been shut down by RBC. Azamara asked if I would call the Bank in the morning and sort it out. A call to the number on the back of the card put me in conversation with a person in one minute, who, after a few introductory questions, determined that the ATM transaction in Zanzibar, Tanzania was suspect (perhaps by an automated process). Within a few minutes, the card was reactivated. This is not meant to be an advertisement for RBC...only that I read it as a positive attribute for the protection of my credit when abroad. I also learned, coincidentally, while reading Matt Ridley's book, The Rational Optimist is and I quote: 'Whereas it takes a handful of steps to set up a business in America or Europe, that to do the same in Tanzania would take 379 days and cost $5,606. Worse, to have a normal business career in Tanzania for fifty years you would have to spend more than a thousand days in government offices petitioning for permits of one kind or another and spending $180,000 on them. Little wonder that a staggering 98% of Tanzanian businesses are extralegal."

This morning we decided to relax on board, read more of Ridley, and enjoy a luncheon BBQ by the pool and make ready to sail toward Maputo, Mozambique at 17:00 with all systems go.

Another beautiful morning awaits us, then a surprise, Captain Filip announces 'whales off the Port Side' and passengers and crew head for the sighting. Terryl saw them but I didn't.

Last night a very funny Comedian/Magician entertained a packed house while using several passengers' necks to insert swords and other instruments to regale his audience. One of the necks belonged to an Aussie and the other to a Teacher who corrected his 'Barbara and I' to Barbara and me' and got a great laugh for her work.

We are at sea all day and have selected a few items of interest to attend: a lecture on Maputo, Mozambique; a Jump, Jive and Swing brand new group of singers and dancers; a Wild Jewels enrichment seminar supporting foundation benefitting Kenya's young people; and finally an Opening Night Party at 22:30, all of which will be time well spent.

We have some information and the history of Maputo, Mozambique (the Capital of a Healing Nation) to share. We dock there on January 15, 2020.

Maputo's population is 1,100,000 with another 14,000,000 elsewhere in their country. The current President is Filip Jacinto Nyusi elected in 2015, with their last President Samora Machel dieing in a plane crash in 1986. The crash appeared to be caused by opposing political views coming from South Africa.

In 1974 a military coup had overthrown the Portuguese dictatorship of Marcelo Caetano to achieve Independence in which they were not ready. In two years there was a civil war and 1 million people died. Frelimo forces ran the show with the backing of the Soviet Union with a peace agreement during the fall of the Soviet Union. Today the country has evolved into a more Democratic-Socialist process of government.

In 1791 the Portuguese took control with a rather superior attitude over the Indigenous who were forced to live outside the city in a slum named Mafala. The governing Portuguese built a state-of-the-art Railroad system and Station (in Maputo) in 1916. [Take note that poorer countries lack quality and fewer Railroad Systems in the world according to 2020 statistics.]

Gustave Eiffel, designed and built all Tin and Steel houses here - can one only image how hot they would be under the sun's heat.

Perhaps Jose Craverinha (1922 - 2003) is their hero who was a great athlete in his day, as well as the poet of Mozambique.

All land is the property of the state; one can own the building but not the land it sits on. And of course this hinders investment and promotes a lack of building maintenance with the state taking the building when the lease expires. All of this has made Mozambique into the second poorest country in the world; corruption is rampant, and slums and dumps are significant in Maputo.

Lastly, when the Cyclones hit the flooding is severe without the necessary infrastructure, but still, there is the odd Luxury Hotel peaking out of all of this.

Today is another sea day, however, Azamara has put on a display of procedures, processes, and day-to-day activities in all departments, all of these are miniaturized throughout the Theatre.

Last evening was a major treat for Terryl and me; the invitation to dine with Captain Filip and his wife Nicola was formalized and in our mailbox asking us to meet with his four additional guests in the Mosaic Cafe at 18:15 for a little sparkling wine and our first toast. The Captain and his wife look like they just stepped out of a movie scene; he is as handsome at 6'5" with a neatly trimmed black beard and black uniform as she is stunning in a beautiful one-piece white snuggly fitted jumpsuit and long blonde hair. The evening was wonderful, the food and wines were superb, all served in Discoveries Dining Room with flawless grace by attentive staff over a period of three hours when we made our final toast to our fellow travellers, and to Azamara for the honour bestowed on each of us.

Today is another sea day before we arrive in Maputo, however, a medical emergency for one of the passengers was announced, and that we would be upping our speed to get additional medical attention in Maputo. Furthermore with our current information - as well as new particulars not to be written here - we have decided to stay on board when we arrive in Maputo. Several days ago we had applied for Visas at the cost of $50 each to travel in Maputo and other parts of Mozambique. I doubt that we will get a refund; they need the money more than we do.

We'll learn a little more about Durban, South Africa, this afternoon, and this evening there is another swanky dinner for all of the guests hosted by The Officers of the Azamara Quest.

And another major treat for Terryl and me; last night we were guests of The Ship's Officers and dined in Discoveries Dining Room with Adele who has worked his way into a management position with Azamara Cruise Lines. He's a fascinating man whose birthplace was Casablanca - (the movie with Bogart and Bergman) - that brings in the tourists with Rick's Place and other establishments almost as famous. Adele is a talker and five years away from retirement; he had plenty to say on every question, but especially on the one that asked, 'When on the tour of the inside's working departments, do you see the living quarters?' His answer was quick and decisive - No, and for all the right reasons such as privacy for people who are front and centre for most of the day and night. Again, the food and wines were superb and delivered flawlessly by Tin (yes Tin), a skilled waiter just like Adele once was, and has trained Tin to be.

We are docked at Maputo, Mozambique this morning with Visas paid through the ship's internal system, however we've decided not to go ashore for the eight hours we are here. Maputo does not have a good reputation. There is more corruption, crime, uncleanliness and other undesirable traits explicitly expressed by several authorities on board. So the plan is to get a full tank of gas and get on our way at 15:00 and boot it to Richards Bay in South Africa. We will sail right under a massive bridge built by the Chinese not so long ago.

With a wake up call at 06:00, room service breakfast at 06:30, and my walk to the Cabaret to see South African Immigration officers at 07:30 and be ready to board my bus to the Game Reserve, everything stopped cold. Captain Filip is on the horn apologizing for the Pilot's helicopter being a little late, additionally, that the Immigration Officers were going to be little late. The Captain also said, "What can you do, this is South Africa?" My read on all of this is not a fault of Azamara…so be calm, get in the line and relax. Many of my fellow passengers followed a different thought, and after a few abrupt words to line jumpers here and there we all left 1.5 hours later than expected.

My tour consisted of a two-hour air-conditioned bus ride to the Game Reserve, a two hour 4X4 (ten-seater) ride through 230,000 acres of mountainous waist-high grassy land with indigenous trees and plants to munch on - for the animals of course, and a two hour ride back. We saw White and Black Rhinos (they are the same greyish colour depending on the soil and water in their habitat), gigantic Cape Buffalo about the same colour as the Rhinos, Warthogs slopping in a water hole's mud and, two different breeds of Antelope and lots of birds, some of which eat the parasites right off the Rhinos's backs. Others saw Zebra, but no one mentioned Giraffe, Lion or Elephant to make up the Big Five.

Terryl did not wish to do this tour because she's done it before on real Safaris that went on for weeks.

My guide was a rather muscled young woman with eyes like a Hawk after having done this work for 17 years. She'd quietly yell out

'Warthogs at ten o'clock.' because she didn't want to spook the animals or us in the back seats. This reserve is not a zoo; everything is all about nature, predators and prey, water and food and seasonal mating.

We arrived back on the ship at 15:30 (1.5 hours later than planned), and for any who were hungry the main Dining Room had remained open.

Last night after an evening meal Terryl and I found a front row seat in the Cabaret to hear an Aussie play a Guitar and a Didgeridoo, both instruments were backed up by Igor's five-piece orchestra. Bruce Mathiske's music was marvellous, however I was pooped from those six hours doing the Game Reserve and couldn't wait to get back to our room and hit the sack.

Today we have docked in Durban, one of South Africa's largest cities. We hopped on the Shuttle Bus to a centre complete with the usual shopping, and things like sea world and other family amusements all reasonably close to one of their dozen coastal beaches. Our idea was to use a local bus for a three-hour tour of the city, but after a half-hour taxi ride getting to the bus we decided to nix it and return to the ship. Around 15:00 three monkeys climbed the ropes and boarded the Azamara Quest and went straight for the Navigational Deck and take control, to no avail. These little guys are a common sight in and around Durban.

At 19:00 tonight, we will be on an Azamara-sponsored complimentary tour to Durban's Cultural Centre for cocktails, a Zulu original dance exhibition, a few nice words by Captain Filip and Cruise Entertainment Director Ernest, and then the half-hour ride back to the ship. At 22:00 The Quest leaves for Port Elizabeth, South Africa.

For several reasons upon visiting the venue for the Zulu presentation the decision was made to host the event on board. It was a smash hit. The dancers and music makers were incredible as they moved about and thumped the hell out of a dozen drums. Along the way, delightful young girls painted warrior-like images on faces of willing passengers: me included. I have a close-up of my painted mug.

Today is a sea day where there will be a lecture 'Rounding The Cape' at 14:00 and another appearance by Bruce Mathiske who we hope will be playing his own guitar and didgeridoo at his 20:15 performance. I failed to mention that his instruments did not catch up to his flight, and that he borrowed a guitar from Igor's trumpet player, and, found a Didgeridoo in Azamara's music vault. Of all the good luck, his instruments have been found and are being shipped to Cape Town just like the rest of us.

This afternoon at 14:00 we'll have a lecture on Port Elizabeth and Cape Town provided by Chuck Richardson who, in forty-five minutes gives only the broadest strokes of their history with some present-day evolvement as two of South Africa's major cities.

"In 1814 the British take over peacefully, and the Dutch were rounded up and sent out of Cape Town to go east in Africa where the Xhosa, principally Indigenous lived. The British demand that Dutch is not to be spoken. Gold and Diamonds were the drawing card to South Africa. Cecil Rhodes organized De Beers in 1830 and pulled three tons of Diamonds (equal to 14.5 million carats) out of one mine in 1873.

The most famous present-day African is Nelson Mandela who had been a terrorist, was jailed and finally released February 3, 1990 to spearhead anti-apartheid protests and in four years apartheid was eliminated by the African National Congress (ANC) and took power. Life is so much better today where Port Elizabeth's population is 1.3

million, with whites at 9% of the population. Still, half of the total population lives on $5 per day.

Cape Town's folded mountains, Table Mountain, Devil's Peak, Signal Hill, and Lions Head highlight its unique topography. During Britain's hey day in Cape Town the Indigenous were allowed to own a total of 7% of the land. I'll close with these comments: South African penguin are unlike Antarctica's and are declining in numbers, Right Whale can be seen, Ostrich are common, Architecture is of course principally British and Dutch, Stellenbosch makes great wine and the waterfront is a safe place to be. I'll find out about one of my primaries when we get there.

Last night our friendly Aussie Bruce Mathiske played brilliantly, and during a pause in his music he alluded to several conversations he'd had around the ship. Wouldn't you know he was asked why he only wore socks, without shoes, while he played. "It's because I didn't want my constant toe-tapping to be heard by my listeners." Makes sense to me.

Azamara displayed a chocolate fountain, a dragon sculpture in chocolate with trays and trays of chocolate goodies for everyone as they left the Theatre.

Today we are in Port Elizabeth and docked. We decided to take the shuttle to its drop-off point and see the sights. Frankly, it disappointed us: there were few people there and the crafts and art didn't do it either. The WiFi was terrific and I cleaned up a lot of business on the computer, at which point we left and returned to the ship. Of all the warnings we have heard, there have been no incidences, until today. Two of our acquaintances, while walking down a street were met by a Security-dressed person who told them he had free tickets for them. He asked them to follow him, they did and when they arrived at an ATM two additional persons arrived on the scene and told them to insert their card and to do the obvious...both of these older people started screaming and successfully ran away from these crooks. We're told that Cape Town is much better than the other South African cities that we have visited. Let's hope their recommendation holds water.

Tonight another party called 'The White Night Party' begins right after 'The White Night Buffet' at 20:00. Clearly, everyone is asked to come in white clothing. I've got a long sleeve silky white tee shirt which will fit right in.

Last night the aforementioned White Night Party rocked. First, a fabulous meal, second, 12 locals dressed in Native Costumes sang and danced up a storm, and then the Entertainment Team took over with two hours of red hot music that were meant for dancing. They were terrific, the energy they have and with most of us dressed in something white amidst floating white balloons the night flew by as the seas bounced us around even more than the music.

This morning had to come, we are sailing around The Cape of Good Hope in choppy waters, all having been forecast with a recommendation to take the patch that helps with sea sickness. Terryl was talked into taking one - I didn't think I would need it, and so far so good.

We'll be packing up tonight, and when morning comes we'll leave the ship and taxi to Mount Sierra Apartments in Cape Town.

In the morning, we said our goodbyes to all, including our Captain and left the ship on a beautiful sunny morning. A taxi was within yards of the gangway and we're on our way to the hotel.

After a seamless checkin with Chantal at Mount Sierra Apartments, we hopped into a comfortable one-bedroom, fully furnished, fully equipped kitchen that met our needs perfectly.

We are off on The Hop On Hop Off bus (this is routine for us in any new city) and from the city centre on the Blue Line head southeasterly on Rhodes Drive (Cecil Rhodes started De Beers and his world-famous uncut diamonds from South Africa in 1844). We drive around Devil's Peak past Kirstenbosch and their National Botanical Gardens to our first stop to catch the Purple Line to Groot Constantia Wine Estate established in 1685.

Groot consists of 763 Hectares of land granted to Simon van der Stel. With slave labour, he established this place which today is the quintessential South African Winery making 25% whites and 75% reds all in French-made Oak Casks with Portuguese Corks - no screw caps or boxes sold here. Terryl and I enjoyed a tour of the estate and of course, a wine tasting that excited our palates and our knowledge all supplied by Jacques. The tour of the wine making and storage was given by Victor who was attentive, a little funny and a wealth of information. I asked about one of Terryl's favourites: an unoaked Chardonnay? And he replied oh yes, but we never make it at Constantia. Our casks are made in France with French Oak.

We continued on along the southern coast past Hout Bay, Camps Bay, Clifton, Bantry Bay, Sea Point, Three Anchor Bay, Mouille Point and off at Victoria and Alfred for some food and walk-about (shopping). We are going back to Camps Bay tomorrow.

And so we did get off at Camps Bay and did a little walk-about and then sat down for a cool one. We are across the street from a magnificent sandy beach reaching 100 yards into emerald green water. On our side of the street there is one café after another and all of them appeared to be prospering on a sun-drenched gorgeous day. However, we had plans in Victoria & Alfred waterfront and off we went to buy some tickets to the Nelson Mandela Museum (and his prison for years) for January 25, 2020. The museum wanted to see our Passports and said in no uncertain words, bring them with you on the 25th or you'll be denied boarding for the sail over to Robben Island. We had a full day and this cough that came out of nowhere, except that Terryl had it for a week, is wearing me out; we hopped into an air condition newish taxi and told him that Chantal (of Mount Sierra apartments) wanted him to treat us very well. We were in his Donat's cab for twenty-five minutes, Donat, from French Guiana, is his name, and the cab fare was 850 Rand ($8.50 Canadian).

Up bright and early with some OJ, coffee and fruit for breakfast, and down to the lobby where Chantal asked what's up today. She called Donat for us and the three of us went to A Gem Store operation, secretly displayed in their driveway, and let them know we were here. The buzzers went off and in we go with Donat waiting for us while we looked at R250,000 (that's $25,000 Canadian) diamond rings and necklaces for twenty minutes. Terryl simply stated that she wanted to think about it for a day or two. Of course I said okay and we politely excused ourselves and proceeded to the front door and out to greet Donat. Because of my nagging little cough I thought better of playing 18, or even 9 holes on Rondabosch golf course but that didn't stop me from going there, entering the pro shop, buying the Tee Shirt, asking for a right-handed 7 iron, going to the driving range, hitting 5 balls with my new Adam Bazalgette grip and swing, and in 25 minutes we went to the parking lot and hopped into Donat's car and left to go to the magnificent Mount Nelson Hotel, only two blocks from ours.

This place is steeped in tradition and old-world style, comfort and tried and true service. We casually walked in and with Terryl at the helm they were all over us with an escort showing us around inside and out. I finally sat down in a nicely shaded easy chair while Terryl cruised with a camera in hand. When she returned we ordered a glass of local Chardonnay and beer: both were fabulous with some nuts, olives and chips served complimentarily.

Our next stop was Tom's Mozambique and Portuguese Restaurant just up the street from Mount Sierra apartments. This was lunch consisting of 3 glasses of South African white and a shared plate of Seafood &

Spaghetti. We loved it, and all for the cost of R250 or $25.00 Canadian. Life is good down here. I hope you have felt that as you read.

This evening we ate at Café Paradiso only 50 yards north of our luncheon. We were served by a lovely young lady named Memory. We hit it off instantly when I said I love your earrings. In a flash Terryl starting talking about earrings to match her necklace purchased in Durban that she just hasn't been able to find. Memory said that she was going to a shopping area that has just what she's been looking for. Here's the deal: she is working Sunday between 09:00 to 16:00 and Terryl will see her and buy those earrings from her no matter what. Pretty nice I thought.

We have an early morning rendezvous with The Nelson Mandela Museum which will include a water ride to Robben Island, where he was imprisoned for a long time. We can't wait to see this valuable piece of South African history.

Donat picked us up and delivered us on time to see a brief moving picture of several of the former inmates including Nelson Mandela. The Tour at 11:00 was a sell out. While we were in line an attendant came to me an invited me to jump the line and take a seat; at first I said no thank you, but two minutes later I was in his offered chair. We boarded a rather large Catamaran and ploughed through calm water for thirty minutes, disembarked, and stepped into one of several buses to start the tour. As we drove a fine young man spoke and referred to us as my Good People over and over again. This place, Robben Island was discovered in 1488 and has had many uses; the most important was to lock away undesirables such as Lepers and Criminals. We passed by the Leper Graveyard with numerous comments from our guide and continued right around the island pointing out building after building and their place in the order of things over all of its history. All of this was labeled Part 1 of the Museum Tour. Part 2 started when we left his bus and were introduced to a former prisoner who had spent

18 years on Robben Island. He stood before all 60 of us and told of the detail involved in sleeping, eating, labour in the Lime Quarry, toilets, punishment and silence which was most important for Political Prisoners who were the last group of inhabitants. The Real Criminals had far better treatment than the Political Prisoners. Nelson Mandela served 18 years with much of it at hard labour in the Lime Quarry where his eyesight was significantly damaged. We saw the tiny cells with a 1/4 inch thick mattress to sleep on, the bucket in the corner, and nothing else in these cubicles. We entered an open sky surrounded by four concrete walls where prisoners and their visitors lined up to talk to each other for ten minutes. They were ten yards apart as well. Additionally, our guide mentioned that much of <u>A Long Walk to Freedom</u> was written between these walls by the one man who is exalted, praised and above all, the man who gave South Africa back to its rightful owners. That man, Nelson Mandela, and the people he encouraged to follow him, had used peaceful means - despite the blows and mistreatment they endured for hundreds of years - to bring about the democracy and well-being that we see today.

Africa is all sorts of people from far away and original coastal regions, and with the migration of Africans from the interior to feed the Slave Trade, the coast of this great continent is now heavily populated. The Continent of Africa lost 25,000,000 men, women and children caused by the Infamy of the Slave Trade. The people that we have met on our journey are kind, friendly, fun loving, and go over the top to please. I said that to two black men that we were talking with, and one of them said straight out, "It's in our blood."

Today is the penultimate day in Cape Town and we wanted to do something relaxing and enjoy some fine wine and food. We were in Donat's cab heading to Cape Grace Hotel for a little look around during the noon hour. It is spectacular, with its Dutch roots and architecture in full display: attendants holding the doors open with a big hearty welcome, and two receptionists in place to answer any questions one may have. Terryl asked for a little tour before asking for the nightly rate. The receptionist happily took us around and when we returned to her desk, she hesitatingly discussed the rate with questions like the type of room required and when that would be because the rate depends on seasonal requirements. Basically, it was from 9,000 to 15,000 Rand per night. Divide those numbers by 10 to have the equivalent in Canadian Dollars. We thanked her for her help and information and quietly left this beautiful place right on the Waterfront.

Only 100 yards away is a Food Experience place that looked enticing. All sorts of different foods by different vendors in a pleasant lively atmosphere was a good start when we dropped into a Sushi Place with various coloured bowls circulating on a moving platform. We ate two dishes costed at $10 Canadian, enjoyed it and continued to explore. We stopped for a drink at Gingha restaurant and bar with outdoor seating and umbrellas. We spent three hours having cold ones and a little food; it was perfect and Terryl excused herself for 30 minutes to buy those exclusive earrings that will be perfect with her African styled hanging necklace. (Memory couldn't find just the right pair no matter how much she tried.) All is good and we left for Lord Nelson's Hotel and a final look at their beautiful huge Nassau Pink Verandah leading to a lovely garden and more sitting areas for their guests. It was the end of a perfect day.

It's another weather-perfect day in Cape Town with a temperature around 22C, an approximate temperature for their winter time. We have been on this journey for 49 days and I'm a little tired; we know that we have seen and learned about parts of the Globe that I had thought I would never see. Now if all goes as planned and prepared for we'll be on an Emirates flight this evening at 18:25 and land in Dubai at 05:55 on January 28. We have a booking in the Dubai Airport's 'sleep and fly' for 7 hours only, and then find Terminal 1 for our Air Canada flight at 23:55 arriving in Toronto at 06:05 on January 29.

When I'm in my chair in Port Credit with my Cozy Desk and a hot toddy and biscuit in hand, I'll start to think about our trip and attempt a summary of sorts. But then, is a summary necessary? Perhaps we'll be on another adventure while the snow flies in PC.

We are indeed in our chair with Cozy Desk on July 4, 2020 reflecting on the specifics of our trip. Some said they enjoyed following our journey and that they enjoyed my writing as well. To that I credit my days of study at Arthurs Jones as well as York University and the zillion books I've read in the last 75 years.

My mind works in mysterious ways. It finds detail to key on and never sway or let it wander until the job is done. I think that aspect of my behaviour helped when attention to detail is the only thing you should have on your mind. And then from time to time it wanders, and now is one of those times.

Chapter Nine

I'm jumping back to my university days that started after 41 years of working in the Printing Industry where I grew to love and cherish the people and skills that created and produced beautiful documents with beautiful words in diamonds of black type for all of us.

My first contact was when I called York University after returning from Wimbledon in August 1998. I telephoned administration to apply for enrolment in an English Literature course. After a few minutes on the phone the woman said thank you, and, asked me to write a two-page letter outlining my life's experiences after leaving Riverdale Collegiate in 1957. I wrote that letter and mailed it the next day. I'm disappointed that I never saved a copy. Two weeks later, the phone rang and I said hello. At the other end was Professor Koretski from York U who said, "May I speak to Gary McDonald?" I then said, "This is he." The professor was blown away with this grammatically correct response and went on for several minutes about the beauty of the English language when properly used until he finally said, "We want you to enrol and I will be at the head of the class with a much younger Trevor Holmes assisting me as the T.A." This wasn't night classes for adults, I was in with the recent high school graduates during the day at York University. My brother Richard would have been proud. My university-aged sons were speechless and I couldn't wait to get started with Professor Koretski.

After a few months of reading Virginia Woolf, Jane Austen, Geoffrey Chaucer and James Joyce I was eager to put a story together and chose a character named Miss Q.R. Ramsbottom. You see Miss Ramsbottom is a fictitious radio personality operating in the UK early in the 20th Century and she has invited Leland Bondfaig to play Virginia Woolf's father Leslie Stephen on her program. This is it word for word:

Ramsbottom Takes on Virginia Woolf's Father on the BBC

This is a 1927 BBC radio-staged drama/interview of Virginia Woolf's father conducted by the inimitable Miss Q. R. Ramsbottom. [The deceased noted editor and critic Mr Leslie Stephen is admirably recreated by the aging and rebellious actor Leland T. Bondfaig.]

--Good morning Mr Stephen, thank you for agreeing to participate in our program today.

[So starts the seemingly benign interview of a man who unwittingly provided numerous nasty personality character flaws permanently imbedded in the main male character of Virginia Woolf's recently self-published novel, To the Lighthouse. Mr Stephen had arrived at the sound studio the morning of March 20, 1927 determined to set the record straight, to defend his honour, and to challenge his daughter Virginia's recollection of fact and family life in the Stephen household. Soliciting sympathy was a daily occurrence for Mr Stephen; and everyone knew how difficult single parenting was especially with a most difficult awkward young girl who adored her mother—may she rest in peace. His plan was to prove conclusively that he was a misunderstood but able Father, not the feared manipulative strict authority figure his daughter had delivered to the world—and all for the sake of her idea of art.]

--You must be very proud of Virginia, her book has taken London by storm, and everyone is proclaiming her style and technique to be uniquely different and innovative in a novelist's approach to writing; they predict Lighthouse will become a classic in the world of Literature. Her novel actually reads like poetry, don't you think?

--I don't know about that—she certainly didn't follow any style of any book she found in my library. I always encouraged her to spend time reading literary masters in the hope that she might learn from them.

--Oh Mr Stephen, I think she has. Her use of language is melodic and passionate as it is complicated and colourfully dense—I think you'll agree, I'd like to read a passage if I may?

--Which one?

--The dinner party starting section 17.

--Fine, go ahead, I'll be listening carefully for the density.

[The lovely and talented spinsterly-looking Miss Ramsbottom had been a mainstay in the BBC's Literary Department. She loved her work, especially when the requirement to read aloud (her passion and delight) would have her voice fall on all of England's ears. She cleared her throat, adjusted her skirt, loosened her already loose tie, and took a small sip of clear liquid from her glass and began to read ever so slowly, verifying and creating the soft flowing introspective dynamic shaped by Virginia Woolf's syntax.]

--"But what have I done with my life? thought Mrs Ramsay, taking her place at the head of the table, and looking at all the plates making white circles on it. 'William, sit by me,' she said. 'Lily,' she said wearily, 'over there.' They had that—Paul Rayley and Minto Doyle— she, only this—an infinitely long table and plates and knives. At the far end, was her husband, sitting down, all in a heap, frowning. What at? She did not know. She did not mind. She could not understand how she had ever felt any emotion or any affection for him. She had a sense of being pas..."(Woolf 89.8)

--Now stop right there, Virginia is dead wrong about her dead Mother and, in this book even me! How could she feel and say those things putting unkind words in her mother's mouth? Mrs Ramsay, I mean Mrs Stephen and I had a wonderful marriage and she adored me, and I took care of her as a gentleman must a lady.

115

[Miss Ramsbottom was visibly shaken by Mr Stephen's outburst and reached for another sip of liquid. Two more required coughs from Miss Ramsbottom followed by her soft lilting but now determined voice.]

--I'm sure she did Mr Stephen! You are Mr Ramsay in <u>To the Lighthouse</u>, and if so, then I must read from another part of the same section to make the point!

--Of course I am, all of the places, all of the settings and all of the family members are mine.

--Then I'll begin, "Raising her eyebrows at the discrepancy—that was what she was thinking, this was what she was doing—ladling out soup—she felt, more and more strongly, outside that eddy; or as if a shade had fallen, and robbed of colour, she saw things truly. The room (she looked round it) was very shabby. There was no beauty anywhere. She forbore to look at Mr Tansley. Nothing seemed to have merged. They all sat separately. And the whole of the effort of merging and flowing and creating seemed to rest on her."...(Woolf 91.4). Mr Stephen, why does Virginia describe her mother's feelings in the dining room this way? Was the atmosphere as depressing, and the responsibility of socializing and intermingling as she writes in the balance of that paragraph, all hers? And I could point to numerous occasions where the children fell victim to your mood, shall I?

--Miss Ramsbottom, it is truth to tell, that because of <u>To the Lighthouse</u> it is not current common knowledge that my wife and I were very much in love. Through Virginia's eyes and her memory of those days the opposite might seem to hold more certainty; however, with the benefit of my well-adjusted mind, I confirm that Mrs Stephen was a remarkably beautiful woman in many ways, and, that Virginia at one time yearned to be just like her. Here, give the book to me I want your listeners to hear a particularly accurate feeling Virginia had about her mother and me.

[The sound of turning pages filled a 15-second void while Miss Ramsbottom stared at her bookless hands.]

--Ah yes, here it is and I quote "He turned and saw her. Ah! She was lovely, lovelier now than he had ever thought. But he could not speak to her. He could not interrupt her. He wanted urgently to speak to her now that James was gone and she was alone at last. But he resolved no; he would not interrupt her..." and Virginia venerating our marriage continues, "And again he would have passed her without a word had she not, at that very moment, given him of her own free will what she knew he would never ask, and called to him and taken the green shawl off the picture frame, and gone to him. For he wished, she knew, to protect her."(Woolf 72.5). Miss Ramsbottom, I loved my wife and my children, and I did everything within my power to protect them. What else could I have done? Here! Look at this photograph I have of Virginia, she was 21 years old at the time, is she not beautiful? My job and the agreement I had with Mrs Stephen was to protect her and the children—and that is what I did. Virginia should not have said those awful things about me in this damned book.

--Do you think Virginia loves you Mr Stephen?

--Yes I do. But I realized long ago that she loved the memory of her mother more than me—and, more importantly—more than any other person or thing or place in her thirteen-year-old world. And she would like us to believe that she never forgets anything, anything at all? When my wife passed away Virginia was heartbroken and depressed. Anyone would expect that, but in Virginia's case it was far too long a period of time and had a devastating effect on her. She seemed to turn inward and sought solace and solitude in, and only from my library. I let her have complete freedom with my books and she read and read and read everything there was to read except my work, and my books. She seemed happiest when she sat down to write. She's a clever girl but I don't think her plan to write on subjects like male/female relations, something they call the struggle of the sexes, family effects on children, her own experiences, life versus art and a host of other things—that she thinks people will want to read—will place her work in high esteem. Do you think her book would have been published if she had been forced to seek a publisher as I did? I don't believe I'm wrong here, what good did it do James Joyce when he wrote that abusive trash about his family and the schools he was fortunate enough to attend in <u>A Portrait of the Artist as a Young Man</u>. What good did it do him? He's done nothing since; he lays about in Paris doing God knows what! At least Virginia is publishing books and now that this one is in print, I'm here to wish her and her husband Leonard every success with the firm.

--Well Mr Stephen, the fullness of time will best provide the answers to your questions, and when the tally is done, the portraits of Mr Joyce and Mrs Woolf as artists will then be obvious to all of us.

[Miss Ramsbottom turned her torso slightly away from him, raised her rolling eyes fourty-five degrees toward the ceiling, readjusted her skirt, drank the balance of her glass of clear liquid and spoke directly into the face-sized microphone.]

--On behalf of our audience and myself, thank you Mr Stephen [and Mr Bondfaig] for setting the record straight and sharing your views on your daughter and her work. And to you, the discerning listeners of the BBC, please write, we want your comments. We feel that we have an exciting author in Virginia Woolf, a woman who pens her most intimate, darkest, and loving feelings fearlessly in a refreshingly bold and decidedly different manner. She has an independence that no other female writer has ever attained; I think her writings will make a better world for everyone who reads her, especially women. Please send your letters to: Miss Ramsbottom in care of: The BBC, P.O.Box W.O.R.D.S., London, England. Thank you for listening. Good day and good reading.

Work Cited

Woolf, Virginia. To the Lighthouse. London England, Penguin Books 1992

Joyce, James. A Portrait of the Artist as a Young Man. Penguin Books (U.S.A.) 1993

Stephen, L., & Ramsbottom, Q.R. (Producer and Interviewer). (1927, March 20).

The R in Ramsay has the Last Word. BBC

Miss Ramsbottom came to life when I sat down to write the above story. Q.R.R. is a fictitious character to be sure that Alexander McPope had nothing to do with. However, Virginia Woolf and Leslie Stephen are real, just as real as To The Lighthouse is to modern day English Literature. When Miss Ramsbottom straightened her skirt and took a sip of her Gin before speaking into her microphone, *"We feel that we have an exciting author in Virginia Woolf, a woman who pens her most intimate, darkest, and loving feelings fearlessly in a refreshingly bold and decidedly different manner. She has an independence that no other female writer has ever attained; I think her writings will make a better world for everyone who reads her, especially women."* she spoke for half of the world's reading and writing population who yearn for the freedom that comes with the printed word.

Now is a good time to introduce an article we wrote after I left Arthurs Jones and business, and began working on the last part of my life and a happy retirement?

Chapter Ten

*T*he following column appeared in the trade journal
*'PrintAction' in July 2002. When Gary was asked by the editor
Jon Robinson to wrap his head around the Baby Boomers
phenomenon and predict how the printing industry may change, or
not, as a result of the demographics of Canadian society in general,
Gary collaborated with his son Rob and they came up with this weird
title:*

Dot Lovers Versus Pixel Peepers

In the fullness of time, printers as we know them—I'll call them dot
lovers—will bend even more and give way to the onslaught of
computer technology. The power people of the computer world—who
I call pixel peepers—want to convince the dot lovers to leave more
and more words and images on the screen for viewing by their target
audience. As letterpress yielded to lithography and mechanical
assemblies disappeared under the vicious and sudden Mac-attack of
the 1980s, many traditional methods and providers of print are part of
Canada's social and economic history.

Big printers get bigger while commercial printers fight for survival in
a duel of the ubiquitous print broker/trade printer combination. A clear
example of this battleground was the caverns of Manhattan in the mid-
1980's where the owner of a web press, without a single employee to
his name, manned the phone by day to find a few guys to run his
machine by night (PrintAction, December 2001).

The above may have relevance to those strategists who relentlessly
pursue all things wonderful except their next printing orders, but
today's thoughtful business planner looks to the future to decide,
which path will bring them the riches they deserve and expect.

Technology changes, but let's not forget that people change as well. The human drive for technological change will always force its way into the marketplace, but it is also vital to realize how demographic shifts can alter the arena. The population—coupled with its technological following—provides clues to survival and prosperity.

There have been countless examples illustrating the rapid adoption of technology by the consumer. Trends that are too often taken for granted. Consider that within the past few years nearly half of the households in North America, instead of a tuned-in few, now use the Internet. A White House report states that 700 new households in the United States are being connected every hour. The same reports state, that since 1995, more than a third of all U.S. economic growth has resulted from information technology enterprises and more than 13 million Americans hold IT-related jobs, and the rate of growth is six times as fast as overall job growth. At one point in this amazing growth Bill Gates so aptly pointed out that the world now buys almost as many PCs as colour TVs.

People access information from a computer screen where there are a gazillion pixels that need no translation onto paper for reading or archiving. Saving your documents is just a click away. Sending to another pixel peeper is just a click away. Learning -- just about anything you want to know -- is just another click or two away. Buying is a visa card number and another hesitant click away. Investing is yet another nervous, but certain, click away. The clicks will eventually become more and more a part of our lives, just like the stinky noisy automobile rose despite the familiar clip-clop of the insouciant horse's hoofs on cobble stone city streets in the twentieth century. And it will be the consumer's accessibility to the technology—like the sudden mass production of the car—that leads this industrial change.

According to Statistics Canada, in the year 2001 there were 2,716,000 Canadians between the ages of 55 and 64. Stats Can's projection into

2006 for that same group is 3,651,800, in 2011 there will be 4,329,600, in 2016 to 4,839,900 and the 2021 projection is 5,127,900. That is a percentage increase of almost 90 per cent over 20 years when the total population of all age groups will jump 16 per cent (31,081,900 to 35,381,700) over the same 20-year period.

The century's aging superstars will be everywhere, both in and out of the workforce; this august and demanding group will resist massive changes and insist that the world be presented to them on paper. And they'll have it their way, and why not, these greying citizens will be custodians of the lion's share of the wealth in this country. They'll be invested in the old economy while tampering, they'll tell you courageously tinkering, with the new economy. Give them their newspapers, annual reports, travel brochures, advertisements for cheaper and more powerful computers, instruction booklets on how to do just about anything and print it on paper just as it has always been.

Market your services to this group of aging, but healthy, consumers as they flourish in their remaining years. They'll be buying upscale cars, looking for the latest cure for their trick knee recently re-injured on the tennis court, buying the best health can offer in food, drink and advice, and of course the condo and the vacation package to-die-for will be on their lists. But, keep a sharp eye on the younger generation—with their increasing purchasing power as they inherit and create their own wealth—and follow their parents in business and society looking for processes that are BETTER, FASTER and CHEAPER. They always do. And this is how I see the future when the trend to an older monopoly begins to reverse itself around 2026:

Every scrap of information is created and stored on a computer. Everyone who reads has a computer. Years ago our magnificent Canadian banks had reduced their normal paper transaction costs from $1.48 each to $0.04 each for electronic transfers of our sacred money. These kinds of electronic savings will now dominate the process of buying and selling; we'll be ever so close to a cashless society.

Instructions on how to build or repair anything, where and how to travel with an e-ticket and all the classic or trashy books we wish to read are described, opined and ready to ship in an instant are only a click away.

Huge conglomerates, various industry leaders, followers of the better, faster, cheaper ideology have discontinued providing the magnificent glossy printed annual report to their shareholders and followers. Now after years of begging its customers and shareholders to let it be so, it's here, it's all on the Internet. The demand for speed needs the systems already in place and begs for more of the same—only better and faster. Film has already been 'bettered out of existence.' How fast will the press makeready actually get?

Slowly, but surely, more and more pixels will stay as pixels and not be converted to dots for plating and printing on paper because it's just too slow and costly based on the return on investment in more, but not all cases. Text and imagery will be available exclusively on the screen. The men and women who manipulate images and text on their computers, along with its owners and clients, will dictate the media used to transmit the message. Oft times more than one media will be used to garner an improved response, but only until the best pay back media is absolutely known to the seller.

The companies that understand the most profitable media for their customers will be Canada's multimedia tycoons and earn enormous riches as a product of their wisdom. Printing on paper will be glorious, almost reinvented by the process of de-selection, where original art, photographs and text are chiseled, manipulated and saturated with colour alongside the jewels we once knew as diamonds in black type. (30)

Writing the article just read gave me a warm and agreeable feeling, so comfortable and enjoyable that I asked PrintAction if they would like another. They did. And if you wish, here it is:

123

[But first, I thought this altruistic article would speak to a general concern of mine for the Industry that provided me with everything I enjoyed during almost all of my working career. I loved working for my co-workers, clients and suppliers. I was paid a significant commission or salary for those last thirty-three years of my time in the business and I wish the same for those who made the same bet on Printing as I did.]

Trade Printer/Broker: Changing the Face of Printing?

When did it begin? Was it the Mac attack of the middle 80's? What is different about the printing business? Is it because the tradesmen work without the ever-present, proud and immutable ink under their fingernails? It's a fact that the unseen work produced by the printer is primarily conducted in a clean environment. Gone is the Linotype and the Low Slugger found in the type house; the traditional, as well as its replacement type house is typographical history. Film and plates are made using the continuing science of invention and completed by a near-hands-off process. The use of a wrench is without purpose on the heavily laden electronic printing presses of today. As a matter of fact, a printer with a wrench in hand is a major problem for the production-hungry employer—the manufacturers of these $5,000,000.00 printing machines say so, not me. The suggestion that the craft has become a science, therefore, requires considerable scrutiny. The argument made by the equipment manufacturers is a valid one: press the right buttons at the right time and you've got images; you've got film and plates— if you really need them—and you're printing in minutes, not hours, not days.

The process is vastly different than it was fifteen or twenty years ago; however, the most important factor changing the face of the printing industry is not the printing process, that honour goes to the men and women who direct the business affairs: the owners of the equipment. In my view, it is the role and responsibility of the investors of capital, the ones who purchase the machines, and to whom they report, that have changed the face of printing.

On a business trip in the early 1980's, my partner Duncan McGregor and I visited a printing company in New York City; we also wanted to see the operation of a particular piece of press equipment we had an interest in. The great printing companies—to our dismay—didn't exist in New York. By great, I refer to a company housed in a large, attractive and functional building with lots of employees, all sorts of different presses doing elaborate work for big name clients that are the envy, or, if you will, that set the standard to which lesser known printing companies aspire. As a part of our day trip, we visited an office tower housing print brokers. The tower was down the street from a printing company that boasted of one employee and one machine. The employee was the owner of the company and his machine was a half web; the people required to run the press were not in the building that morning. While this scenario appeared bizarre to us, the owner confidently said, "by eight o'clock tonight this baby will be running; I'll find a couple of guys who'll want the extra money, I always do." The paper, plates and ink would be shipped to his plant during the day under the direction of a broker who worked in the 'Tower'. And the following morning, the printed stock would be shipped to the bindery of choice. That was the plan; we weren't around long enough to see the results. That was our first experience with a New York printer/broker combination. I concluded that no one with a large investment in the Printing Industry had any contact with the original client—in this case anyway, it was rent-a-press by the hour or the night.

Who took the ultimate responsibility for the completed result? The printer had the machine—was he responsible for the final product? I presumed he really wasn't. The broker fed the materials to the printer and then to the bindery—was he responsible for the final product? I supposed he was; but would he be financially responsible if something had gone wrong? I thought not; after all, his investment was his time and ability to convince the client that he could deliver as promised. If these suppliers didn't, he'd call someone else to get the job done to his satisfaction and find fault with the original suppliers' effort to avoid payment.

The trade printer was born in The Big Apple a long time ago. The big companies with the employees and the reputation had fled the Manhattan scene. I understand from more recent dealings that they have prospered as a result.

I see that the trade printer/broker concept permeates the pages of PrintAction. Are they today's dominant player in The Big Apple North? They appear to be the prevalent advertisers in PrintAction; are they paying for the ads in a timely way? Are the best and brightest of the printing sales force self-employed as brokers, or, does the printer employ them? Are the profits that are necessary to replace equipment staying with the owner/printer who invests, or, with the broker who has little interest in equipment, but invests their time looking for the best available price, quality and delivery from its stable of suppliers? If it is the latter, and the owner/printer can't afford the ever changing technology, or, chooses not to participate in the high stakes game that is, or was his to foster and feed, then the face of printing will continue to change into a something like the New York entrepreneur who mans the phones by day looking for someone who needs the extra money.

Doing business directly with the company who has the original requirement for printed goods and services is good business for those who seek and find it. The people who understand the importance of this concept and implement appropriate action by and for its people, will change the face of printing in the big-apple-north. Is it the broker/trade printer combination or is it the commercial printer who will set the standard for the Industry? Who is running the printing industry today, and who is benefiting the most? Who would you rather be?

Watch out Heidelberg. (30)

Chapter Eleven

W e've spent plenty of time printing, playing and learning about life up to this point. I hope I still have your attention because this next part of me is real, and that is being a father. It may not be for everyone, but for me, I welcome and cherish my days and nights as Greg and Rob's father.

Greg is 53 years old and Rob is 49 this year and of course, my role has evolved with the passage of time. When they were older, they joked with me and we laughed at my athletic endeavours requiring trusses and leg tape when I was on my way to the courts. Dads can have good times with sons as little guys too. I sure did when one of them rode on the back of my bike down the street onto the Beach's boardwalk, running with our dog and laughing all the way to the hot dog stand. Our dog was BeeGee named after his owner Rob: B *for Bob*, G *for Greg. (Bob changed his name to Rob when he left home.)*

Bob, at eight years old, brought a puppy home from the Pet Store on Queen Street, which was just around the corner from our home in Toronto. Three days later, Greg carried a kitten home from the same store. BeeGee and Septima (the kitten) were inseparable, chasing each other all over the house for two wild weeks. Finally, they settled down and realized that they would be sharing with the four of us for the foreseeable future.

BeeGee went to obedience school because we were told that was the thing to do. Septima purred around the house and danced to her own tune without the advanced education that BeeGee was commanded to absorb. I didn't like the program, and I think BeeGee hated it. Could the trainer's technique be alien to the breed? I suppose BeeGee's aggressive behaviour could have been choked out of him by the chain around his neck. However, no one in our family was willing to put in the time and BeeGee must have been relieved when this torturous training stopped.

Don't get me wrong; BeeGee had his quiet moments, even when he was young. He could sit still for a while and seemed to be content. I liked to see that in him; but I also liked to see him run like the wind chasing a bird or retrieving a thrown ball. On one of his wild runs, he ripped through our hallway to greet the person climbing our front steps; he was running out of control and slid head-long into a beautiful piece of stained glass splitting it in three pieces. Luckily it didn't shatter and he wasn't hurt. So the glass was never repaired, and he never lost his footing when running to greet someone at the front door again. We lived a stone's throw from Lake Ontario with its' beach and boardwalk, where and when these fun-filled moments were possible. I think BeeGee loved it when he was free to run like all-get-out. His ancestry and he were bred for it. I now think that he had other attributes.

I think that he was an unconditional love for all of us, especially if you gave him your undivided attention. When I look back, I can't say that I was overly generous in this regard. Bob and Greg were good that way. Ours was a normal home consisting of two parents, two sons, a dog and a cat, and one goldfish. That's seven - in Latin it's Septima - and Greg called it a great name for the cat.

As we all grew older, some of us slowed down a bit. The boys left home to attend University, shortly thereafter Anne Marie left home to start a new life returning to single-status. My brother Arch moved in with me and BeeGee and Septima. The years passed as my hair grew grey and then to white; the knees and hips weakened; BeeGee slowed down and Septima was delivered to Greg and his growing family in Quebec City. Now there were three of us.

BeeGee was eighteen years old when his body started failing but he soldiered on with Arch at home and me still selling printing and generally doing just fine. But life was changing, which it always does and one day, Arch called me and said he thought it was time to go to the veterinarian for the final time. I called Rob at U of T and told him that BeeGee needed help. Rob understood. BeeGee had helped all of us grow in character and in life. He was a wonderful gift when some of us didn't realize the value he brought to our lives.

When I looked into his eyes, I saw a being ready for anything. If he could speak, I could hear him saying, "Let's play. Let's eat. Let's go for a run and maybe we'll see a bird or pigeon on the rocks. Are you okay? Did you have a bad day? Come on, let's go; everything will be okay." I never heard him say, "Where's Bob and Greg?" I know he was thinking it.

Pu is like un-carved wood: it's the Taoist concept of being effortlessly, naturally one's truest self. BeeGee never changed when he was with Bob and Greg; he only grew older. He was Pu. I can see that now.

In 1985 my family with Anne Marie and sons Greg and Rob had discussed a move to a new home closer to my work. This new place would have all the current convenience appliances, large sleeping and living quarters and a swimming pool in a yard surrounded by treed nature only. We would have a pool table in the finished recreation room at 1500 square feet directly under 3000 square feet of living space with a walk-out to the landscaped back yard. This place was our version of the perfect family home with a Marley tile roof expected to last more than fifty years. All four of us agreed, and so we had it built and moved to North Brampton in July 1986.

Our home soon became Party-Central for family gatherings and holidays we eagerly hosted. During those years I was content and happy with my life and family. I thought we were flourishing and reasonably challenged with suitable goals for the future. Bob was in high school and growing like a weed. He tried out for the Rugger team and made it. He was in with pretty regular guys, growing, learning and doing fine. He also changed his name to Rob, possibly because he thought it sounded mature. Greg was Go Train and Bussing to UTS in Downtown Toronto and back to Brampton at night for the next two years. During the second year he quietly asked me if he could have an apartment in town close to UTS. I was selfish and told him that I wanted him home for just one more year. Greg and his pals Hogg, Meek and Chris known as the SciGuys, aced their work and delivered the Valedictorian speech for the graduation class that year. During all of this I had bought shares in Arthurs Jones and was enjoying my work that paid me more than I ever could have imagined when I first met Alf, Andy, Scotty, Vic, Ken and Herb at LithoPrint. I believed at the end of my working time, the four of us would walk into our future lives with comfort and satisfaction.

In 1988 Greg was the first to go. The University of Toronto accepted his enrolment in their Physics programme, something he'd always wanted since graduating from Grade School in Toronto at thirteen years of age. Greg was ready to bite off a large amount of life and there was no stopping him.

There are joyful (and sad) times that came to our family of four while living in this house for eight years, but things really changed in the Spring of 1994. It took my wife six months to convince me that we would be happier if we separated. We talked about it daily, consulted a marriage counsellor weekly, until finally I agreed she had to be right. We engaged the lawyers to assist ending our twenty-five-year union. Her lawyer lived three houses north of us; and he recommended a lawyer that lived a mile away for me. Nothing was contested. She would receive half of our total assets and savings, and a nice cheque every month for the next seven years.

In two additional months, Anne Marie went off to re-start her life as a single woman on October 28, 1994. Greg left for Quebec City the day after he and Marie Lou returned from Japan to continue their studies at Laval University and most importantly, to share their lives. In

September, Rob moved to his place close to the University of Toronto to study Architecture and Graphic Design. He had apprenticed all summer with my architect friend Tak Tanaka and was eager to leave home and get started just like a young man would want to do. And I had our dog and cat, my work with AJ and golf at Brampton GC.

My oldest brother Arch had had a few bad breaks in his life, including recently losing his place as a master printer with a firm he had been with for the last thirty years (bankruptcy was the culprit). Arch and I concluded our discussions five days after Anne Marie left my home with her Separation Agreement in hand. Given that, I asked Arch if he wanted to live with me in my very large and almost empty house. He did so in November 1994 and so did I for the next 21 years until 2015.

It is best to focus on good times. There was plenty of that all centred around cooking, eating and socializing. Greg and Marie-Lou, with their sons Ben, Nate and Thomas visited often from Quebec. Rob and my brothers-in-law Garnet and Buster, sisters Joan and Marilyn and their children, and their children's children, and Mom and Dad came to our place where we had as many as 28 people for dinners and 50 or more for a stand-up feasts prepared by Arch and me. The Air Canada group consisting of Terryl's fellow flight attendants and pilots partied a few times every year with Terryl being a big part of all of the arrangements. She loved those parties especially the summer ones that rocked inside and outside our home.

Those 21 years were sublime, but I took ill in the summer of 2015 with a variety of issues and almost simultaneously, Arch fell terminally ill and passed away in November 2015. He had had cancer and he thought he was just getting older. He was only 76 and his last days, I'm sorry to say, where very painful but he drove to the YMCA every morning arriving at 6:30 for his workout and coffee session with his pals until he said his last goodbye. Archie had many years developing friendships with that early morning group of guys.

In 2017 I sold my home of 31 years, and a carefully considered decision was made for me to take up residence in a senior's assisted home with nurses and three squares a day. I had been in and out of the hospital for two plus years, and, I still wasn't operating on all cylinders. The ladies of Rivera Greenway made sure I had my prescription pills and took them religiously. For eighteen months, Terryl came to see me all the time, Greg and Rob followed when they could. I was slow and lethargic and just getting along, but by 2018 I had put my mind and body together rather successfully—with Dr Sayeed's help—and asked Terryl if she still wanted me to live with her. She said "yes" enthusiastically, and I moved into her Port Credit apartment in November 2018. That day was 20 years and one month after our first date.

I am looking forward to my life with Terryl and my boys. Greg, Marie-Lou and their sons Benjamin, Nathan and Thomas live in a beautiful home built for them in Shawinigan Quebec, and Rob's apartment is in downtown Toronto where he is close to his work and friends. Both have made good decisions regarding work and abodes.

I began this story in 1941 living on Curzon Street and will end it on High Street East in Mississauga South just a few days before my Last Will and Testament is read.

These nine addresses are in chronological order: 94 Curzon Street, Toronto East _ 110 Jones Ave, Toronto East _ 204 Wineva Ave, Toronto Beaches _ 45 Victoria Park Ave, Toronto Beaches _ 80 Scarborough Beach Blvd, Toronto Beaches _ 36 Fernbrook Crescent, Brampton North _ 100 Ken Whillans Drive, Brampton South _ 70 Park Street East, Mississauga South _ High Street East, Mississauga South.

When in Toronto, we live on High Street in a 3 bedroom, 3 washroom, 1600 sq. ft., 12th floor Condo with a wrap-around large balcony facing south and southwest to our beautiful Lake Ontario, where it looks and feels like home.

When we are not in Toronto, Terryl and I will probably be on a ship cruising around places we have enjoyed before, but miss very much. These words cast my mind back to Terryl's burning desire to travel anywhere and anytime with Garfield (Gary) Leonard McDonald and constant invisible companion, *Alexander McPope.*